Cocaine Poet Part III
Junior Junkies

Leon J. Gratton

Grosvenor House
Publishing Limited

This book is published by
Grosvenor House Publishing Ltd
Link House
140 The Broadway, Tolworth, Surrey, KT6 7HT.
www.grosvenorhousepublishing.co.uk

This book is a work of fiction. Any resemblance to
people or events, past or present, is purely coincidental.

A CIP record for this book
is available from the British Library

ISBN 978-1-80381-610-4

RIP Dad

Chapter 1

Grandad hated fucking school. He wished he didn't have to go. But he and his crew were a dab hands at the violence game and the amount of people who wanted to play with them (against and for) was unreal. They were never there, they had challenges to meet, drugs to take and beer to drink. But school was for fools they registered in then fucked off. They had punters to handle and as usual they came first, business as usual, the selling of tarrie, speed, eckies and coke. They would dive upstairs and deliver the Class A's first, then the rest was dealt with by weight and money was flowing into the YBC's pockets, you know they would have sold their stocking soles for the right price. Which was what some young ladies would have offered, but they didn't need anything other than the narcotics.

As party, party, party was the phrase most of the young women stuck to, meeting at midnight with various gangsters. They never gave tick unless it was honoured with Jewellery or antiques, and it had to be rare like Chinese dynasty rare. But that shit was seldom around there, I mean who the fuck wants an antique in the drug game. Nobody that's who. Gramps had done it once and the said item is still on show in his mam's house. A fucking Ming vase. I mean this is Wester Hailes, Edinburgh and it's a tough place to raise anyone. So when he showed up with said vase his mum had ruffled his hair and said, "nice one son." Worth at least a grand he found out later.

He was in his element and made a name for himself, not in smack but in Cannabis and speed. Becksy, Nugget and Beefy had all formulated plans on how to run the drugs on their own without family intervention but Grandad was saving his brownie points with the fucking heads of the Broomie to make a score down in Manchester. Pinkie was still rolling in it from a great score in Dundee. He had parted with fifty ecstasy, twenty strawberries and a shit load of angel hair. At least a half ounce. Pinkie had made one of the best reputations in his area. But he was still loyal to the YBC. He had heard the rumour of Grandad's next big score and wanted in like immediately But Gramps was standoffish and took no crap from Pinkie. I mean this was the competition between the two of them and it left Pinkie a little bit bitter but he got over it. I mean what's another name down in Manchester compared to his in Scotland. Ach he got over it. I mean they argued like brothers and Gizmo had to separate the two of them a few times. But Grandad had always admired Pinkie he liked his flavour, his panache, his mother fucking style.

That style had shown itself not only in the drugs he took and sold but in his clothes, his girlfriends and most of all his capacity for violence. He was a year older than Grandad, But that meant shit when it came to the fights and nights of a Scottish Hooligan. Shimmey had gotten on board with them during the last year of high school, but he had moved from Niddrie to Wester Hailes with his two brothers and their younger sister Lorna. Chris and Allan were the two brothers and they stayed in the background of the scene. They weren't as tough as Shimmey, but they knew he would need them later.

*

Shimmey had a passion for knives and he didn't take shit from anyone. Not neighbours, not police, not even the local chieftains. Oh, he hated one set of people, the lowest form and that was the paedophile the ones that claimed they were gay but all they thought about was corrupting young boys leaving years of scarring and years of bad feeling in families. No, Shimmey had warned a load of them off his friends daughter, Julie, whose Mum was a smack head. But this was exactly his point about money and misery. I mean the guy pinned her and none of us knew him then he ran by like a speeding bullet with half of Wester Hailes behind him, giving chase. Paddy was Jane's boyfriend, he was fast on his heels. Jane being Julies mum.

Anyway Grandad had shown colour about this and no wonder. As it turned out he had been lured into a series of sexual mishaps, which his mother and her friends had sorted out. Sorted out without the dads of the two boys. Grandad had to leave for Manchester as he was not a popular person in the area as he fought and drank, mainly down in Broom toon. His uncle had gone, to school in Broomhouse Forrester High. And Grandad had made it clear he was from Broomie. This had meant him getting the shit kicked out of him by Scott Coleman. Coleman's brothers were in the security business, and that business was clubs. He had a little beef with Grandad who had squared things over with him. It cost Grandad a bullet. That he had filched from Raymond, his mum Lorna's partner.

They had had several discussions over the perversion of a teacher at Grandad's Primary school, Mr Hutchison whom Scott's brothers had beaten up over his corruption of Primary Seven boys. The conversations they had were very fucking hush. Like talking about said people invited them into your families and you were left reeling in the chaos that they had created. Pure Pink Floyd school of thought. The teacher at least had someone holding his leash in that story.

Anyhow back to Madchester, Grandad headed down, still reeling off his Thunderbirds binge and cannabis toking. He was long past the hangover and pain part, no he was munted and nicely, so that's when by some strange shape of fate Danny his cousin and himself, began a nightly vigil of drugs and drink. He went down to Manchester flying the flag of Scotland, proving to, not only himself but to his crew back in Edinburgh, that he was no pushover. He began to mix with the girls and to show that he was ready for the good times, him and Danny started with beer. They were painting his Grandma's house and had been paid a tenner each up front.

Grandad went along to the local off licence and bought a six pack and a packet of fags. His cousin on the other hand had snuck out of his house two king Edward cigars. This was going to be fun, Gramps had thought to himself. He was still holding from just before he left Wester Hailes. Half a quarter of nice Moroccan, or as it was known Rocky. He began to put the skins together and burst the fag right along the crease. He then burned and rubbed the hash into the joint with the tobacco. He inhaled some of the dry hash as it was burning and sending a lovely, sweet aroma around their senses. Grandad added a twist to the joint then bit the wick and lit the spliff. He inhaled the lovely piece of dope and immediately got stoned. He smiled a dopey, goofy smile and handed the joint to his cousin.

"How much have you got mate?" Danny said.

Gramps continued to smile a grin, "just enough to tide me over until I make a connection."

Danny Indian toked it then handed it back. Gramps fisted the joint and blasted the cobwebs from his dull wits, he took another swig of his beer. Danny sank his can of lager and lit up his cigar.

Gramps was nicely sozzled and toasted with the joint. "When you gonna introduce me to your dealer?" Asked Grandad.

Danny smiled and let out a few smoke rings. "All in good time mate, all in good time."

Danny and Grandad carried on with the task in hand. But they drank themselves into a stupor and had to abandon the work. They then went and had a severe attack of the munchies. This was all well and good but Grandad who was muscular and had a huge appetite was known for Biscuit and Jam pieces. Grandad had a good rest that night, summer was just kicking in. The hot balmy air in the village of Prestwich was a sleepy little place, with a couple of boozers where the locals drank to their hearts content. The place was idyllic, one of a kind, people knew each other and most people spoke to each other. Grandad was a bit of a fish out of water. Well, it was going to be fun for him. He woke the next day went straight for the cereal. He tried to keep on top of his hunger as it was a make or break situation with a dope fiend. If you had the poppy you could live like a king. But when the beer ran dry and the dope went up in smoke. You just had to count your blessings and one of them was a healthy appetite. I mean if you were constantly hungover and vomiting, you know somethings wrong with you. Hangovers are usually excessive alcohol. But a whitey, a whitey would run its course and you would end up with a nice stone after the sickness had gone away. But it wasn't all roses and wine, no you had cunts coming from the sidelines. Threatening, wanting a piece of you, trying to get in on your action. I mean small time draw is small time draw. But Grandad was like the heavyweight champion of dope. He was a force to be reckoned with. He was cooed and ooed over by the girls. And the laddies in that area were warned off him. He was immediately sent back a year because the curriculum of the local schools was different to Scotland. Grandad felt very cheated by the whole English system. But in his heart he had longed for Scotland. Homesickness. But the deal was still to be finalised and a lot of toking, smoking and joking was on the menu.

Chapter 2

Grandad ate his cereal in silence and listened as his Nan rhymed off about rules. Home by ten or locked out, leave the mars bars as she was diabetic and needed the sugar fix. Always shower, help with the housework. Pocket money was, well it was being negotiated. Grandad's dad would try and be through once a week. This too was under negotiation.

Danny appeared that morning smiling and singing the Happy Mondays tune 'Step On'. Grandad smiled as he loved it and loved it and loved it. Today they were meeting with a couple honeys at one of their houses. Where they would drink Merrydown cider and toke some dope. They made their way to the hunnies home, and began to joke, toke and soak their sins. Simone Howe, whose house it was, walked over to Grandad and sat next to him, "You'll be Leon?"

Gramps smiled looked into her blue eyes and said, "Aye doll, I'm Leon."

She smiled and giggled a little. "It's your accent," she said and then smiled, "It's strong and thick."

Grandad smiled and replied, "Aye rough as well."

She giggled a little. "Could you do me a favour?" she said, "Could you set me and your cousin up for a cop off?"

Grandad smiled took a swig of his lager got up and walked over to Danny, "Danny boy that lass wants a bag off with you. You up for it?"

Danny smiled, "Yes mate, definitely." He then got up took her by the hand and headed up the stairs. Grandad walked over to one of Simone's pals and said, "You're alright want tae head upstairs?"

She smiled at the young casual and said, "Yeah sure, you got a condom?"

Gramps laughed and said, "Aye doll I always carry a johnnie."

They then headed up the stairs to the master bedroom, where what wasn't long, but was just enough to satisfy the pair of them.

"I mean it could have been worse, I could've got brewers droop," Grandad said later, saving face.

Then Simone after finishing with Danny said, "Danny thinks he's in for it with his mum."

Grandad smiled and said, "I've got a braw idea."

He then lifted Danny up and took him to the bathroom. Grandad then got all the girls to strip him off and sober him up. Grandad went, "gurgle, gurgle lucky bastard." He sobered up then went home.

Grandad phoned his cousin later on it was answered by his Aunty Carol. "Hi Aunty Carol."

His aunty smiled and shouted up the stairs. "Daniel its Leon."

Daniel leapt down the stairs and said, "Right mate, how you doin'?"

Grandad smiled his pearly white teeth, "Sully I'm grand," Danny waited then replied, "Thanks for earlier I had a fucking ball."

Grandad laughed a brash loud laugh, "All in a day's work"

"When you gonna introduce me to your dealer?"

Danny laughed, "tomorrow matey, tomorrow."

Chapter 3

Paul rested the paper down after reading the headline, Thirty tonnes of Cannabis seized. "Fuck," he said then popped his head out of the window and spat. "That means we'll be heading into a drought."

The whole of north Manchester was going to dry up. Gregg knocked the ash off his joint and said, "Sully wants to know if it's okay to bring a member of his family for a session?"

Paul sat down and began to skin up, "Yeah course he can."

Paul licked his fingertips, "is it his Scottish cuz?"

Gregg inhaled some more of his joint. "Yeah man," he continued. "What's his nickname again?" asked Paul.

"Grandad," came the reply from Gregg.

Ollie who was sat there gouching and coming down from an acid tab piped in, "Grandad?"

"What fucking kind of name is that?" he continued.

Gregg smiled and returned to his joint, "You know what Scots folk are like Mad," he said then passed the joint over to Paul.

Paul roached it then lit up the one that he had just built. He could use some cheering up, he thought as he bit the wick of the spliff and blazed, it crackled slightly. He had made it part slate part really dry grass or as it is known bush. Paul inhaled the joint for a second or two.

Then passed the doobie to his left, Ollie took the spliff and sat down against the wall. "Put some tunes on Ollie."

He looked at the tape cassettes that was near to the Hi Fi. "What do you wanna hear?" he asked.

Paul smirked to himself, "Some reggae, put Bob on."

Ollie smiled and produced Bob Marley and the Wailers *Legend*. "When is this mad jock coming?" Paul asked as the tape player played 'Stir it up little darling stir it up'.

Gregg took a few more tokes then spoke "Tonight I think." He then passed the joint to Ollie. The song changed to 'Easy Skankin, "excuse while I light my spliff spliff. God I really need a lift".

Paul smiled and sat down on his bed. And began to skin up another. Crushing the very dry bush with some slate or red Leb, He was thinking about this Scot. He knew they were no grudges between him and any Scotsman but the guy according to his supplier was to get the golden treatment. And that made him slightly wary. But Sully was a good punter and he never brought the law to his door. Not so far. Anyway night was drawing nearer and Danny and Leon arrived at Paul's door. He opened the door and smiled at the two Blondes that were stood one with a slight tan and blond surfer cut hair. Cut into a French crew cut his labels weren't too bland either Sonetti, Lacoste and a pair of British Knights trainers. Danny was in Levi 501's, a Teddy Smith T-shirt and a pair of Timberland boots. Paul smiled then jerked his head to motion them up the stairs to his den. They got upstairs and Paul said as he closed his bedroom door, "There's a drought, as you can see," and he pointed to the newspaper, and the photo of the lorry filled chock-a-block with cannabis resin, a street value of thirty million. "So what we have should last until the next load gets through. Which in all things being relative should be about three or four weeks".

Grandad smiled as the music set the ambience the mood with Floyd on at first then some Doors. Then our mate Marley. To finish things off Temptations and 'Papa was a Rollin' Stone'. This was Paul's favourite Motown song. They all began to chat sizing each other's habits to see how far they could stretch a gramme of cannabis, sometimes they made bong mixes or had spatzes (Hot knives). Then Grandad realized it was time to go home and rolled one for the stroll as he needed to stay in control. That was when grandad decided to see how fast Paul could roll, sixty seconds sometimes three or four seconds sooner. But he had his own record, Blowback closest to the roach wins. He roached four out of five. He got home and rested with his Walkman on and listened to the Happy Mondays *Bummed* was his favourite album of theirs especially the song that went, "Daddy put your house up for sale the Indians are coming." He sat in the small room with a dooberon lit and stoned music to his ears Happy Mondays

*

The next day he awoke, the sun light shining in his window sparking the little room into gold. He was in narcotic bliss. He had reached Nirvana with very little effort. It was a fine morning and Grandad had places to be, people to see and then he would be ready for that nights festivities He bought some cider and some lager so he could make snake bites. Tip a little out the bottle and fill it up with Lager. And it had to be Merrydown cider and Skol Lager. The girls drank Lambrini or Diamond White cider. They were fond of their wine, whereas Grandad loved his narcotics. And he never let go of that part of his own personal heaven. Dope and pussy, he was forever coping of with girls. He went to Simone's house first collecting money to purchase, what they call in Edinburgh cargo. A healthy night on the razz. With smokes and dope. They were all going into Heaton Park after Grandad had scored a sikie from Paul a sixteenth of hash it was slate but he would have to make do as the haul that just got busted. Was meant for the north end of Manchester. But it would flow again sure as anything it would flow properly as an abundance of the stuff. It was like turning on a tap that had air locked. It would cough and splutter then whoosh a full sink ready for a bucket. The dope just had to get back into the system. It was even more accessible with the police running around catching nothing,

"Couldn't catch a cold," was what Breenie would say. Breenie was one of the local lads who no one would mess with, he was at least 18, 19. Built like a Mafia hit man. No there were growlers then there were growlers. Breenie had a thing for grinding his teeth when his habit was too much. And you gave him your tarrie just to be on the safe side. "Skin up Breenie!" then toss him your lump of dope as he was fine, sorted, you know the guy had sit downs in Spain and France. He was a part of a gang whom I can't mention here. No, not at present. Simone and Danny wandered off into a small spot that they kept secret. Grandad hooked up with a heavy metal chick Called Emma. She was juicy and bubbly and a total screw, but she also had a boyfriend. This didn't bother Grandad as it made the chase more thrilling. I guess he hoped she would pack him in, but alas no, Grandad was looking forward to a fight with the guy.

*

Grandad spoke about his crew in Edinburgh and his mates. But didn't want to cause any friction between him and not only the local lads in Prestwich but the crew Grandad belonged to. I mean he was winging it so far. His connections were about to kick in and make him very popular with the local talent (not that he wasn't already you know his broad Scottish accent). No, he was about to become well minted he knew of several fishermen that were bringing in ecstasy and coke. He was coming up in the world. His friend and writer Liam Burnett was about to deliver a great big stash with a couple of bundles of Northern Lights grass. This was being hidden up north and was waiting for the call. Grandad took Paul Kelly aside and explained the amount of dope and the money involved. Paul smiled and said, "as simple as that."

Grandad smiled at Paul and replied, "As simple as that."

Paul looked around and huddled him into a corner. "I've got a rat problem."

Grandad snarled a little, Paul continued, "It's an out of town problem."

Grandad looked at the dealer. "An out of town problem what do you mean boss?"

Paul lowered his voice, "Several people have been and went, whilst me being foolish I have accidently dropped names of some of my suppliers. They were busted right on the nail. Now I know you I know your family and I know they have a love hate relationship with the Law."

Grandad Stopped his thoughts from consuming him, "You are going out on a limb with me." Grandad smiled, his pearly whites out. "My cuz says you are no fuss and definitely no fuzz."

Grandad produced a joint and blazed up. Paul looked around and thought this guy has it all planned. But that was a Scotsman for you always had a big idea, then with his idea he would make a thousand little ideas which would roll into one big idea that would sort him out for life. Paul liked him even more. The night sailed on and Grandad got a lot out of that talk. He even managed to stay an extra couple of hours.

Chapter 4

The next morning, he got up, lit up and headed downstairs to the front porch where he smiled and took a drag of his Benson & Hedges cigarette. He then went and made himself a brew. Yorkshire tea. He sipped the mug full of utter bliss, you know the bliss that comes down to a well maintained habit of drugs and drink. The season was summer and it looked like Grandad had struck it rich. He phoned up Pogo, "How yae dain man?" said grandad.

Pogo smiled, "Am dain no bad Gramps."

Grandad, "We are about to strike it rich Pogo, montey money."

Pogo smiled, "Me and Liam will be down just before school is back for new term."

Grandad punched the air, the excitement was bursting out of him. "I've already lined up the buyers."

Pogo stopped his bird in the hallway, "Get us a can of Lager doll," he then whipped her behind with the pad of paper he was holding.

"Viki!" He shouted as she walked away "Love you."

"Aye yer a chancer Pogo."

Pogo smiled at her, "what was that doll?" he spoke back.

"I love you to, dear!" she shouted back

Pogo carried on writing down the numbers that Gramps was reciting. The good thing about Leon was that he was good with most numbers. He could put them to memory and five six weeks later he would remember them when the time was needed. He had a mathematical brain and was good with numbers. But the fact that nothing lasts forever. Well that was a thought that he would contend with when the problem arose. Grandad put the receiver down smiled his in his most charismatic way just as his nan entered the room. Of course she knew none of the details that Grandad had been planning. But that was for the best. The less she knew the less likely she would come to harm if it all went sour.

"Awright Nan?"

The small frail woman had something to prove and she bit at him and bit sharply. "You ate my Mars bars."

Grandad cursed at himself, "I know Nan I'll nip along to the shop and buy you a new one."

She sat down and Gramps said, "I've just made a pot of brew you want one?"

She gave a little chuckle, "Yes well that would be nice."

Gramps went through the kitchen and poured her a warm, strong brew. He took it through to her and waited for her to really have a go.

"I want a whole bag of Mars bars you're not getting off with it lightly. And it is coming out of your pocket."

Grandad smiled and said, "Ach nae bother nanna I got enough left over from last week."

She smiled and carried on drinking her tea.

*

Danny walked up the path to Paul's house. He knocked on the door and waited. Paul came jumping down the stairs. "Alright Danny?"

Danny put a fag to his lips lit the thing and said, "I'm sound mate, sound."

Paul jerked his head in a come up notion.

"Where's Your Cuz?" Danny smiled and thought about the night before and the drugs and drink.

"He'll be around soon," Paul sat down and began to spliff up.

Danny could feel the stone before he even started to toke.

"Put some music on," Paul said.

Danny looked at the extensive tape collection picked out a Pink Floyd album *Final Cut* Roger Waters began to sing and immediately you were drawn into the spirit of music.

"Tell me true, tell me why was Jesus crucified?" the album played on and the drugs began to flow. Danny scored three gramme at about five pound a gramme. Worked at about a pound a spliff. Then the rest of the gang arrived Olly, Gregg, Jimmy Boyle, Breenie and Ian Poland. And of course Grandad. They began the dope session listening to music and playing cards. This went on from half past five and finished around ten o'clock. Then they would part company, Paul would roll his morning joint, go to bed, get up and first thing he would have was a spliff.

*

Liam was dodging about Broomie when out of one of the windows Pogo shouted. "Hey Liam?"

Liam smiled at the guy "What is it Pogo?"

"Just wait right there I'll be right doon," Came the reply from Pogo.

Nichol was just turning the corner to head up to Pogo's bit. "Awright Liam?" he asked and then continued, "Got any Ganja?"

Liam smiled and said, "Nah man what do you think I'm here for?"

Pogo came out the stairwell Buzzing out his nut, super hyped. He began to spraf at a tremendous rate. "You know we are on Liam."

Liam kicked himself, he had forgot about the Northen Lights deal. It was coming into fruition.

"Manchester," He said and took Pogo's hand and shook it.

"Grandaaad," Came Pogo's response.

Liam smiled and scored straight away, "It's on the house."

Then Pogo handed him a quarter of dope and three gramme of sulph. They were wraps not bags. Bags were smack and they weren't made like a letter. They were small usually made from half a skin. Easy to conceal but a nightmare if you lost one. Nichol. Smiled at the two of them.

"Gies a lay on Pogo?"

Pogo smiled at Nichol, "all I got is a sickie left."

"When you goin tae pay me?" He asked.

Nichol smiled. "The morrow when I get paid for the Juice wagon."

Pogo smiled at Nichol who was making a drama out of nothing

"Okay, okay, okay but dinea haw me chasin you the morrow," Pogo lit a single skinner of top grade hashish that was black, red seal.

"Well?" asked Nichol.

Pogo handed him the lump, enough for seven and a half joints.

Liam smiled as the deal was finalised. "Are we going to Pinkies for a session?" said Liam.

"Aye Barry. Liam, is Pinkie in?"

"He should be," replied Liam, "His mam and dad are working and Gizmo is waiting for me at the library."

Liam smiled then got passed the single skinner. He took a big deep inhale of the joint. And gave the rest to Nichol.

Nichol smiled smelling the rich dark tarrie smoke of dope. "Yeah!" he said as he inhaled the smoke. The day was sunny and worthy of a Bob Marley song. They headed off to the library and then went to Giz and Pinkies house. A small house that housed two adults and three children. Pinkie answered the door before Giz had chance to open it with his keys. "Awright lads?" he asked then they all piled into the sitting room.

They began to pull out fags and skins and wraps of speed. Pinkie came through the room with bottles of Becks. They began to spraf and get drunk. The neighbours didn't say a word. Teenage angst and alcohol fuelled frenzy yeah they had a lot to be thankful for. I mean teenagers huh. This was the height of summer and it was fucking brilliant. Whilst Grandad was getting fucking wasted. So were his hombres. I mean when the deal was made Gramps would be rolling in it. Pinkie smiled as the conversation got more and more intense and the jokes and joints passed themselves around. They finished all of the beer then started to crack into the spirits. Giz dived off and got some Lemonade and cola. Enough to last them till the Adults came back.

They rolled the last of their dope then Liam headed back to his house in Calder. He was staying with his aunt. The rest dispersed. Back to their den's and homes.

*

Grandad and Paul dropped a couple bombs of speed. They then waited for said narcotic's to kick in. They began to get on each other's wavelength spraffing faster and faster. This went on for five six hours. Grandad was more and more munted. Adding alcohol to the mix, mainly cider, kept the high that the two of them were on at an even level. You could say the two of them were fast on the way to being friends.

Grandad asked Paul quietly, "You sort that rat problem out?"

Paul smiled a joker-toker smile and said, "I have my suspicions."

Grandad looked at the ground and said, "You tell me when to make a move, and the deed will get done."

Paul smiled at this, showing his wicked shark like smile. It was slightly unnerving to Gramps but he handled it with cool, calm, stoned resilience. He knew why Paul was so respected. He had ice running in his blood, but also a good head for business. And he always kept the punters happy. Grandad smiled and put the skins together for a large cone. And Paul tossed him a lump of slate. It was about a half ounce. Gramps pulled out four fags and began to burst them open. Then mixed the dope in with the tobacco and put it in the skins. The music that was playing was The Doors – 'L.A Woman'. 'I'm the crawling king snake, and I rule my den' was playing with Jim's baritone voice spilling into the room. Every one of them was stoned, immaculate. Suddenly the whole house stopped to hear Hyacinth House. Everybody exhaled there smoke and went, "Yeah" In succession.

'Why did you throw the Jack of hearts away? It was the only card in the deck that I had left to play'. The buzz was really going and going steady. They had a ball.

Chapter 5

Dawn woke from her sleep on a hot Saturday morning, it was muggy and sticky and she was feeling really horny. She sat down and began to pen some more into her diary. Mostly fantasies about being a Casuallet and joining a gang. She had heard names of one of the coldest crews in Edinburgh The YBC. I mean she was spinning whilst listening to stories about certain individuals. Pinkie and Grandad being her favourite two. She loved the fact that they were friends yet bitter rivals at the same time. She lit up after penning in her diary. Dawn then began to listen to 'Atomic' by Blondie. Then she gathered her shit together and headed out the door to her Saturday job in the sleepy wee village called Inverkeithing. She worked in one of the high streets chemists. Often she thought 'You'd think that would make me popular' She smiled, "Someday" She said to herself quietly and walked into the chemist.

John her boss smiled and said, "Morning Dawn."

Dawn smiled and said, "Morning John."

They then went about their business of running a small town Chemist dispensing scripts and Methadone. She saw herself as a no hoper in a town of dead beats. She was sixteen at the time and saw very little hope for her future. She had a small frame with exotic eyes that said, "Come to bed", her raven hair and curvaceous backside made her one of the hottest girls in that one horse town. She was a wee screw but didn't let the opposite sex conquer her easily. No she picked and chose who she slept with and you had to have something other than money. She had heard of Grandad and Pinkie when she was still in High School. She had heard all the stories of the YBC and the kind of gentlemen they were.

But Grandad she really fantasied about. He was suppose to be a smooth operator. A nice kisser with a French twist. A handsome beach bum of a lad. The type right out an S.E. Hinton story. She found herself, after the word got round to her having small masturbation sessions, fantasising about Grandad sleeping with her, sucking, fucking, hugging, licking and most of all necking. She longed for him. But alas she would say to herself, "Never gonna happen" she mused on him some days writing down her fantasies and small poems of lust and love. She carried on with her day.

*

Pinkie smiled and sat down in Ali Greys house, "Pit the fucking *Wall* on man" He said and produced his fags Skins and dope.

Ali smiled and said, "Aye why no." Then put the tape into the VHS machine. *The Wall* began. "It was just before dawn one miserable morning in black forty, four," filled up the house. Rodger Waters at his best thought Pinkie.

"What's Grandad up to?" Said Ali blazing up a nice joint.

"Ah dinea ken," Ali laughed a little at Pinkie knowing that the two of them were inseparable at one point. "Pogo said that Grandad has got a big score of dope and coke."

James smiled at the telly as the music and video were going hand in hand causing a mild trippy state. "Well my man if Grandad has got a big score we are all gonna be a lot better off." The two of them smiled at *The Wall* and carried on toking and joking whilst the video carried on bursting off riffs and guitar solos. The movie was heading for the last part and the two of them were glued with Cheesy smiles on their faces as the trial began.

"Good evening, worm your Honour," came blasting at them. James pointed at the arsehole of a judge and said, "That's Gerald Scarfe at his best, trippy as fuck." It was an Allan Parker film with Bob Geldof as Pinkie. He had made the most iconic masterpiece of film ever and no one can deny it. It left you feeling confused yet satisfied at the same time.

"That space cadet glow," Giz chapped on Ali's door, Ali scoped out the window and saw Giz standing there with a load of booze. Becks and Millers about twelve of each. Ali clapped his hands together and said, "And now my thirst is about to get quenched." He then let Gizmo in. They opened up a bottle each and rolled a joint between the three of them. Gizmo smiled at the joint and blew the hot rocks into the ashtray

"Pit *Scarface* on man?" Asked Gi.

Ali went straight over to the video collection that stretched up the wall. He looked for a second or two then pulled it out. Then he pulled out the tape and replaced it with *Scarface*. They sat down and carried on smoking and drinking for the rest of the day. *Scarface* was moving along just before the chainsaw scene and Ali smiled looked over at the two brothers and said, "Skin up one of yaes."

Pinkie smiled and said, "thought you had a bucket rig?"

Ali smiled and said, "Aye I dae. That's a great idea Pinkie."

He then went and got the bucket filled it and got an old half plastic bottle with Gauze over it and began to make bucket mixes for the three of them. The chainsaw was whirring and cutting into Angel, one of Tony Montana's crew. They made a few buckets each then carried on watching *Scarface*.

*

Grandad lay on his couch in his Nanna's and he was burst, I mean mega come down with a mega hangover. BURST.

His Nanna sat on the chair adjacent the telly, "Go to your bed and sleep it off." She laughed as she said this and then continued to speak, "How the mighty have fallen"

"A Scots lad too, meant to be able to hold their water."

Grandad gave a chuckle, "Aye well," He groaned, "it was a hell of a party."

She giggled some more, "I don't need details my lad, go to your bed."

Grandad got up and headed up the stairs to his room. As he thumped around he began to play, 'Red red wine by UB40'.

His Nanna just smiled and carried on watching Wimbledon.

Grandad fell into a coma like sleep whilst on his tape deck was UB40.

Simone arrived at his door. "Hi Mrs Gratton."

She smiled at the young blond teenager and replied, "Call me Sheila."

Leon was by this time snoring the house down and it seemed to be in sync with the reggae that was playing on his cassette deck.

"Can you give him a message for me?" The young curvy girl asked.

"Yes," was the reply.

She then lit a cigarette as did Leon's Nan. "Tell him that I'll meet him up the fields just at Simister."

Grandad's Nanna puffed away on her Berkley barge pole of a cigarette. "I'll tell him soon as he wakes up."

Simone smiled and put out her dog end in a little brass ashtray. "Thanks Mrs Gratton."

Sheila tutted and replied, "It's Sheila."

Simone walked away saying, "Thanks Sheila."

Chapter 6

Paul was smoking a joint and counting his money. He usually did this twice a month and then went out dancing in the Bury area of Manchester. He had a nice ounce of whizz, that was great and he had enough for the taxi in and back. And Gregg took over the punting side of it whilst Paul had a ball. He was entitled to this at least once a month, I mean dealers get fucked off after a while. No matter how long you have a habit it pisses you off. The same folk round your door always keeping an eye out for the law. It was well, a gilded cage, with it being more than it's cracked up to be. Your habit and your reputation were the only two things you needed and the balls if everything went south on you. You may have to get violent.

Paul use to brag about how Olley and him had found a large sum of money and a firearm. The sum when they counted it was twenty thousand pounds. They had just put there foot in it as one of the local Chieftains had pulled an insurance job and had stashed the money and the firearm, so Paul made his claim by contacting said gangster and he was immediately in the Cannabis trade. Paul had come up from his little pound a joint game to handling bricks of weed and big bags of Speed, Acid and everything. Breenie was in heaven at this he knew the boy that had pulled off the heist. So he got extra's, a sly ounce here and there. Breenie was a madman so was Polland who had warmed to Gramps almost immediately. They had met in a grave yard two weeks earlier and an instant liking had happened. They were full of compliments to each other showing off their tools. Polland had a Rambo knife. It was nothing special to Leon as he had seen his mate Shimmey with one similar. Leon produced a cosh and extendable bar used in the mechanics game.

Polland was at that time seeing a young girl called Claire. Polland had been screwing her for some time and liked to do it roadhouse style, you know a comfortable screw against the wall. He doted on her. She was one of Simone's pals and she was hot. Polland also had a pet in his house, a pet Tarantula. Grandad and himself took to going to town to pick up food for the spider. Crickets mainly. Live crickets, as the Tarantula liked its food fresh.

*

Shimmey was smiling as he scored himself a half ounce. He was going to Pinkies house and he was going to get high, high. He put his small earphones in and started the walk to Pinkies, he was listening to the Stone Roses greatest hits he always listened to them or Bob Dylan. Shimmey smiled as he got to Pinkies door. *"I don't need to sell my soul he's already in me."* Was blasting in his ears. Pinkie opened the door and Shimmey pulled out the lump that was a fair size. "Aye we is, getting stoned san." The lump was rocky and it was the size of a large grape. Pinkie smiled as Gizmo came running I mean they were just about sober. But the night was young and Shimmey had that itch to either fight, fuck or get stoned. Hopefully all three.

"Grandad, the wee cunt is pulling off something big in Manchester." Shimmey looked around made sure nobody was listening. "I think he'll fuck it up. Either end up dead or end up in a YO."

Pinkie laughed a little, "He thinks he is in command doon there but he isnea." Shimmey pulled out a fag and handed it to Pinkie, then handed one to Wee Giz.

They sparked up and smoked "Ach he'll pull it off," said Giz and they all had a fit of the giggles. "I hope so," said Shimmey, "Either that or we all get popped by the top boys."

They giggled some more. "Are we going to Nichols hoose?" Asked James as he put on his £200, pound leather coat from River Island. Shimmey pushed the hash back into his Crombie jacket. And Giz put on his bubble jacket that was a £120 'Kickers' jacket. "Where did you get the weed Shimmey?"

Shimmey did an impersonation of Popeye and laughed. "I got it from a lassie called Tara, she has just moved into Wester Hailes. And I was one of her first Punters, good deal tae, fifty for the half ounce," Pinkie went, "we'll head to Sighthill School roll a couple of Doobies then head to Nichols."

Gizmo smiled at how buzzed he was with the alcohol and drugs from earlier. They sat on the step, it was still light and they had plenty of time left before sunset. Shimmey feeling flush gave some to Gizmo to roll a joint and a slightly bigger lump to Pinkie to roll a better one and he sat down and rolled one for himself.

"Are we gonna go and get Becksy and Beefy?" said wee Gizmo. "And Nugget and Marvin" he continued"

Shimmey smiled a small wry grin "Aye why the fuck no? Let's get oot oor faces." they finished skinning at the same time.

"All together now," Said Giz and they all sparked up. And began to walk into Broom toon. Right past the Sighthill chippy next to the Silver Wing pub. They got to Becksy's door and Pinkie rapped on it and then they waited. Becksy came to the door smiling. "Awright lads?" He asked calmly.

Pinkie looked the guy up and down then handed him what was left of his Joint.

Becksy started to puff, and said, "Any news on Grandad?"

Pinkie whose eyes were slanted like a Chinaman's, "It's all going down in Manchester." He then told Becksy about the score.

"Ach nae fucking way," He said as Pinkie finished off the details.

Becksy smiled at this and said, "There is no way he'll pull it off, He'll end up getting taxed by the local dealers."

Pinkie raised his hands and said, "Aye you know this, I know this. But try stopping Grandad from continuing with the score."

Becksy laughed at Pinkie "It'll be sound if he pulls it off," said Becksy.

They then went and got the rest of the crew.

"Where's Kwami?" Asked Gizmo.

Marvin looked at him and replied, "none of your business." He then walked away smiling at himself muttering, "Cheeky wee fuck." Then he produced a doobie and sparked it. The smell in their wee cloud was sweet. They went in for Beefy, Nugget and Nichol. They then headed up to Liam's house in Calder.

"Awright gadji's?" He greeted them with the Chavi patter. Liam smiled at each of them as they walked into his house and into his bedroom. He looked around them and said, "Tell me you'se arnea all stoned already?"

The question settled on the casuals, Beefy was first to produce his ganja and fags and skins. They then all broke out dope and skins.

"Any beer in the hoose?" Asked Beefy.

Liam scoffed and went "I'll go and see"

Then he went through and saw there were small bottles of French lager. A full case of them. Twenty-four, in total. He took them through and the lads began to open the bottles with their teeth. Biting the caps off and drinking the lager, They then put some tunes on, *Morrison Hotel* by the Doors, "I woke up this morning and got myself a beer, come to the road house have yourself a real ah good time." The album blasted out into the night. Pinkie then put on a gouch classic *Wish You Were Here* by Pink Floyd. Everybody sat down and listened to the hypnotic album, settling their spirits and calming their angst. They just chilled out and relaxed and let the stone wash over them. They sat down to their dope and beer until they were all unconscious.

*

Grandad woke up to his alarm. He was to meet up with a boy called Marshie, he was a local tea-head and wanted to scope out Grandad and the type of dope he was running. Grandad left his Nan's house walked up to Marshie's house and rapped on the door. His sister came to the door and shouted at the top of her lungs, "Marshie, there's a Jock at the door." She then walked by Grandad and headed for the bus stop.

Marshie came to the door, "Just ignore her," he said then ushered him into the dark, dour house. "You got any Puff?" asked Marshie.

Grandad smiled and said, "Course I dae," then sat down and began to build a joint.

They spraffed for the better part of three hours. Marshie was talking about his job as a cleaner in the same yet pub at the top of Simister. He only worked weekends when school was on, but during the holidays he would work most days, "the money isn't great but it gets me by," he said.

Grandad liked the guy, They built up an instant rapport. Grandad left Marshie to go and meet Simone. He saw her pretty as a picture cute with a nice set of tits. She smiled and started the patter, "Hey hey The man from Jock land."

Grandad took her by the waste twirled her around, "Honey you could be a model any day of the week."

She giggled at his patter, But he was serious about her she was a total screw. And Grandad made sure she knew it.

"So what's the big idea?" He asked.

She, smiled then said, "I got a tent we can put it up in this field."

Grandad smiled. "Aye that's Braw" He said then continued, "We could pull of an all, nighter."

Simone kissed his cheek then whispered in his ear with hot and airy breath, "Spin the bottle" He smiled and thought what a turn on she was.

"Aye lass."

She smiled and replied, "We should get cracking". They then went and got the tent and erected the thing in said field. That way they could stay out all night and not have to worry about getting home. Grandad decided later to make a booze run. He went and got a couple of bottles of Lambrini and a couple bottles of Merrydown cider gold cap. Danny came round later to the tent. They began to crack into the booze and few more people turned up. Fiona, Simone's best friend showed up and brought several bottles of diamond white. Danny boy produced a small lump of Puff and immediately set about the task of skinning up. They were in high spirits. Danny was getting nice and toasted. 'A couple more weeks' Thought Grandad and they would have all the money they could dream about. That and a healthy score of Northern Lights Grass. That was getting sold at a tenner a gramme. The real price was sixty an ounce.

Chapter 7

Shimmey woke the next morning He still had a couple of gramme left. And that would stave off the hangover, he smiled as he rolled a nice spliff. The skins wrapping around themselves the sweet cannabis leaving a vapour trail in the air. He put on his earphones and started to listen to Bob Dylan. *'How many roads must a man walk down, before he knows he's a man the answer my friends is blowing in the wind. The answer is blowing in the wind'*. The song was one of Shimmey's favourite.

His brother knocked on his bedroom door, obviously smelling the aromatic vapour of dope, Shimmey growled to himself, "Little fucking bastard."

Chris came in and Shimmey looked at him with a growler. "What dae yae want Chris?"

Chris smiled at him and went, "A toke of that dope."

Shimmey laughed to himself and thought 'Dinnea get fuck all to myself.' He then handed over the joint. And Chris took a few short tokes then fisted a blaster. Nearly roaching it. Shimmey was not pleased.

"Now fuck off!" said Shimmey.

Chris walked out going, "Sorrree." He wasn't sorry in the slightest but that was the whole nature of siblings. They lived to get on each other's nerves and Chris was a dab hand at it. Allan the youngest, showed more respect to Shimmey knowing that things kept good between him and his older brother was the best way to stay ahead in the game. Shimmey walked down to the bus stop and waited 'Time for a new tape' he thought 'Rolling Stones' Was what he was hoping for, *Sticky Fingers* or *Beggars Banquet*. He would decide when he got to Virgin on Princess street. He lit a fag on the bus. Then carried on listening to Bob Dylan. He got into town and procured said tape. Soon as he got out the store door he opened the plastic film and put his new tape on. *Sticky Fingers*. 'Brown Sugar' was the first track. He got back on the bus and headed home to Wester Hailes. Chillin out to the Stones. He got off at Sighthill next to the chippy across the road from Calder and he headed to Pinkies house. James was at the front door having a fag.

"Awright Pinkie?" Asked Shimmey as he drew closer.

Pinkie half snorted half chortled "Shimmey my man."

Shimmey smiled and replied, "Just been to Princess Street, and bought myself a Rolling Stones album.

Pinkie smiled and asked, "A greatest hits album?"

Shimmey shook his head and replied, "Nah man it's *Sticky Fingers* the one with 'Brown Sugar' on it."

Pinkie put out his fag and motioned for Shimmey to come into his house. Giz was still lying half in his bed half out sound asleep.

"Giz wake up," Giz groaned and carried on sleeping. "Gizmo wake the fuck up."

Giz turned over and said, "Sam broon, Sam broon. I'm up"

James kicked him this time, "Up ya wee cunt, we got drugs to smoke."

He lifted himself up and said, "Awright, Shimmey?"

Shimmey smiled and went, "You wanna do the honours?" and handed Giz one he had rolled earlier.

Gizmo jumped into action, put on his Levi 501's, put the roach to his lips then the three of them went outside. Giz sparked up the joint and inhaled the creamy smoke into his lungs his brain instantly going into meltdown. It was a good piece of Rocky. Nice and sweet.

"What's happening with this deal down south?" Asked Shimmey.

Pinkie shrugged his shoulders and said, "Don't know yet."

"Grandad's got some sort of plan and it involves a shit load of drugs," James blew the rocks of the joint before handing it to Shimmey, then continued, "Yeah he's been sitting on the whereabouts of a load of drugs."

Shimmey smiled, "That sounds about right," said Shimmey. "He'll dae us proud."

They then went their separate ways.

*

Dawn smiled as she relaxed at home with a ciggie. Her mum Mary, who was a beautiful buxom dame, smiled at her and said, "You okay Teeny bash?"

Dawn smiled and replied, "Aye I'm okay, I'm just a little bit depressed."

Mary sat a mug of tea next to her, "Ach you are just needing a holiday."

Dawn smiled at her mum and said, "I need to get oot this toon."

She sighed in a sad love struck way. "You've got it bad Teeny bash," She sighed again. "Come on budge up and I'll dae yer nails."

Dawn drew a calm look to her eyes as if to say, 'Aye I know, but I'll live', after her nails were done she wandered upstairs to her room with its Pink Floyd posters, Doors posters and of course Happy Mondays.

"Grandad come to me," She whispered then her hand unbuttoned her jeans and she began to massage her pussy slowly. Right down either side of her labia and middle finger focused on her clitoris. She slowly rubbed her moist juicy pussy and began to build into a moan. Then she reached over to the drawer at her bedside and produced a small vibrator, called a bullet. She moaned and got wetter and wetter until she orgasmed and the sheet was splashed with her cum. She got up and put on some music. It was *American Prayer* that she loved playing. It didn't pull any punches. Pornography, magic sensual bliss righting wrongs and living the beat era. 'My Gang will get you' Then she fell asleep her body longing to be appeased by, someone.

"Grandad." she whispered as she slipped out of consciousness. And into her lullaby's. She woke the next morning to the smell of fried food and tea. She came down the stairs and headed into the dining room.

Her mum was setting the table. "Okay teeny bash tea or coffee, or some fruit Juice?"

She kissed her mam's cheek as she sad this. "Coffee please Mam"

Mary smiled "Two wae coo?" she asked.

Dawn smiled and said, "Two wae coo as per poo."

The radio was playing in the background Kingdom FM the song was 'Strawberry Fields Forever' by Candy Flip.

'Let me take you down coz I'm going to Strawberry Fields'

"The original is the better of the two," said Mary.

"I know, I know, John Lennon forever." she laughed, "things were easier then, people were happier, love was free nobody tried to steal fae nobody."

Dawn sipped her coffee as she listened to her mum spout off about how super the sixties were. Her mum laid down her eggs and bakie. She smiled and carried on listening to her, whilst tucking into a nice traditional Scottish breakfast. That included clootie dumpling and haggis.

*

Gemma came home from her shift at the local Tesco. She was a comely girl but a piece of dynamite when she wanted to be. She would dress so sensual and exotic that men actually fell as they watched her go by. Her pals would laugh at the radges and say things like, "Too good for you ya tube." Then laugh.

She met Liam at a free house where every, one was getting stoned and drunk. They hit it off instantly. Liam didn't lie to her, didn't sugar coat the fact that he was a junky poet and privileged in the fact that he was lucky to be alive. She smiled instantly and every time he was mentioned around her she would sigh. He was just as smitten with her, his pals would joke about him and her. He would get annoyed then when he realised it was just a ribbing, he would smile and send off a huge bellyaching laugh. He was to meet her that night, they were about to paint the town red. Some pubs and a couple of clubs. They kicked it pretty tight dancing and drinking, popping outside to smoke a joint. They really got on well, and never a crossed word between them.

But trouble loomed over the two of them, trouble in the form of a group of Skinheads. The Skulls. They were moving around Edinburgh. Taking from dealers and getting stoned at everyone else's expense. A couple of them were out at the club the Rocking Horse, where Liam and Gemma were. One of them, the head one smiled and looked at Liam and said, "Alright their mate?"

Gemma looked at him as he looked at the pair of them, sizing them up. Liam smiled and replied, "Aye man. You looking to score?"

The young BNP boy fished into his pocket and produced a twenty, pound note. "I want a decent bit of puff. And some speed."

Liam took the money and then promptly produced an eighth of cannabis and a gramme of speed.

The skinhead smiled and said, "I'm Charlie."

Liam introduced himself and Gemma.

"Youse two can dance," Liam smiled and replied.

"Aye we can, we come here every month or so to blow of some steam."

The skinhead Charlie smiled and said, "Nice doing business with you," then walked away.

Gemma and himself stayed in that club till it was about to close. They headed outside to get a Taxi when the Skinhead and three of his Skullheads surrounded Liam and Gemma. Liam grimaced and cursed to himself "Fuck". Then let slip the cosh that was up his sleeve.

"Okay lads we dinea want any hassle." He then in a sudden burst of action, head butted the one that had scored from him. And then struck one of the others with his kosh, knocking him the fuck out, whilst he did this Gemma with a steel bone comb pinned one of the other skinheads against the wall. The fourth one ran away.

The one, Charlie, was picking himself off the pavement. Liam produced a lock-knife and put it to the fuckers neck.

"Gimea my fucking drugs back," he said and the man started to pull out the drugs he had bought from Liam. "And how much money are you carrying?"

The skull grimaced and began to protest but Liam's knife just got that little bit nearer the man's jugular. He pulled out a money clip that was holding what must have been near seven hundred pounds. Liam took it and looked over to Gemma, who smiled and said, "You want me to bleed this one?"

Liam put the money and the clip into his coat pocket. "Nah sweetheart but give him a good kick in the bollocks."

Liam smiled then walked away with Gemma on his arm. He then whistled on a taxi and the pair of them went home to make love.

Chapter 8

Grandad was wrapped in a sleeping bag with Fiona next to him, he rolled over and drew back the sleeping bag that she was under. She was naked and Gramps didn't need a written invitation he went straight down on her. Licking her bald pussy, then when it was throbbing and cum was flowing he got his dick out and fucked her gently. She moaned and grandad pulled out just before he came. Then back down on her. This lasted a good hour. Sucking and fucking, After they finished the romp. They had a cigarette and necked for a while. Then grandad walked her home then headed back to his Nanna's house.

He walked in and his Nan was straight away calling him. "Leon is that you?"

Leon smiled and replied, "Naw it's Jimmy Hoffa."

His Nan laughed a little and said, "Very funny young man, brew up."

Gramps went through the kitchen and switched on the kettle and emptied the tea pot.

"Nan," He shouted through the living room "Did anyone phone for me last night?"

She smiled as her cigarette smoke curled around her. "Oh yes, so there was." She started to think, "some guy said his name was Pogo." She then laughed and asked the forty million pound question, "Is that his real name?"

Grandad let out a giggle, "No Nanna that's not his real name. But thanks for cheering me up," He continued.

Then the kettle switched itself off and Grandad made a pot of tea.

"What is the man's name then and why the devil do they call him Pogo?"

Grandad smiled and sipped his tea, "Your best of not knowing things like that Nan." He then poured her a cup of tea and took it through to her. Then he went and showered and brushed his teeth. He then walked down the stairs in a pair of Peppe Jeans and a Next jumper. His shoes were Hard Rock shoes and cost fifty quid. He put on his Sonetti reversible jacket and smiled at his Nan. "What did Pogo say?" Grandad smiled and took out a fag.

His Nanna smiled, "he said two weeks' time and you and him were fixed to meet up." Gramps smiled and said, "Thanks Nan I'll no be back till the morrow." He then headed back up to the tent. Where Marshie and Ian were waiting for him. They each had a carrier bag full of lager and cider.

Ian was first to hand Grandad a can of lager. "You alright Leon?" He asked and handed him a tin of Skol. Grandad began to chant the advertisement from the telly "Skol, Skol, Skol, Skol," Then a short while later the girls arrived. Claire, Fiona, Simone and Emma. All with bottles of Lambrusco and packs of Diamond white. They all got torn in about the bevvy. Half hour later they were playing spin the bottle and coping off with each other.

Grandad shouted, "Aww fur fuck sakes I'll go and get Danny," then he got up and went to find his cousin. Simone giggled and Gramps walked away muttering to himself. "Shwazafuzacaza ... fuckin" It was Simone's moaning to him to go and get Danny pit a tit right on him. Anyway thought Gramps, he was the best one to have in his corner. He sparked up a doobie and headed for his cousin. He would then saunter round to Paul's house and score a sikie. Then they would be set for the night all that was missing was the tunes. But Danny had it covered. He came down the stairs with a ghetto blaster and a load of tapes.

Chapter 9

Dawn smiled as she walked round the corner to her Job. She was happy, at ease with herself she had learned that Grandad had moved down to Manchester for the time being anyway.

"Lucky fuck," she said to herself, knowing in her heart but hoping in her soul that she would get out of that one horse town. She smiled as she saw John, who was the head pharmacist. And was having a good chin wag with one of the local Grannies.

"Hi John," She said then donned her white overcoat.

John looked her way and went, "Hi Dawn."

Dawn smiled and got the keys for the methadone cupboard. And began to measure it out for the local smackheads. She got a slight sense of importance when she dispensed medicine she knew she was helping heal the sick. She also use to run for the charity McMillan Cancer Support. She did so every year and got many sponsors for the said charity. She smiled and got on with her work.

She smiled as she closed up the shop. She would do the honours Monday morning. She smiled, tonight being Friday she would probably go out with her friends to the local club called Life. She was aching to talk to her pals especially Rose, who was the best one to find out all the juice about Grandad and the YBC. She had a cousin who lived in Wester Hailes, who was going to Forrester High school. He was a young geek called Andrew Lawson.

His dad was a plumber, with his own van and company. He had been seen with friends of Pinkie and Grandad, a friend of a friend so to speak. He wasn't into the whole glory fight for a fun life, yet at the same time sat back and watched as events unfolded. He would then phone his cousin and tell her everything. She would then get in touch with Dawn and tell her everything. But this was all stopped.

Dawn went, "Why?"

Rose took her by the shoulders and said, "You know, things change. He's moved down to Manchester. Probably the best place for him"

"But," she proclaimed, "I was aboot, tae head down there and try to hook up with him."

Rose shook her head and she said, "Look in all honesty I think it's cute you dotting on your bad boy. But he is trouble with a capital T"

She smiled and dried her eyes, "Oh God lass if it were up tae me you would be doon there with him putting a ring on your finger." She gave Dawn a squeeze then they carried on dancing at the club.

*

Danny was blasting the Charlatans, It was about twelve midnight and they had run out of booze and had only a small lump left of hash. Grandad started to skin up. He had gotten himself a bottle of silver cap Merrydown, it was slightly more crisp and tart. But the gold was slightly more sweet. The Doors was next on the tape deck. *L.A. Woman* the album, the song 'L'America'. *A change of weather a change of luck then I'll teach you how to … Find yourself, America, L'America*. The song carried on and then 'Riders on the Storm' came on.

It made you kind of want to get a motorcycle and travel around Britain. Hell even if that was possible they would be better moving to America. Route sixty-six. Bob Dylan, Jack Kerouac, the novel *On the Road*. Jim's Bible in his hand you know Lords and the new creatures.

It was Grandad's dream and he hoped that all his friends were going too, even if it was just to tour. Pinkie had dug that about Grandad he was a dreamer and it was well nice to share your dreams. People are usually looked at strangely when they are living there dreams. Nobody has time for them, but before you got a handle on your dreams you had to have an idea what you are going for. How sane and Insane in the world you were. Like I said people look funny at dreamers. And that kinda sours everybody's spirits. But Grandad had clear vision and determination. Scarface comes to mind, "I want the World and everything in it". But he ended up a back shot coke-head floating in his private water fountain. That ended up filled with his blood. Like his boss had said, "those that fly fast end up dead, keeping yourself straight (Low Key) kept you from ending up dead." Grandad admired the character of Tony Montana. So did most people the fact that he wasn't a worm like the man with the car bomb remote control. Just as he was about to push the button Scarface shot him blew his brains all over the passenger window.

*

Shimmey was getting tired of everybody talking about Grandad. "So what!" he said, "he's lucky."

Pinkie smiled, "I know, He'll see us all alright."

Shimmey shrugged his shoulders and carried on muttering to himself.

Pinkie smiled and said, "Anyhow, he's not the only one who can score big."

Shimmey's jealous streak suddenly subsided. And he was smiling again. They carried on into Broomie, and sat down at the Primary School and began to skin up. They had enough dope to get nice and mellow. Then Nugget appeared with a crate of lager and they began to get pissed. All of them sprafing about how the summer is going to end on a high note. Especially if Grandad sorted out the deal of the decade. If they could get their foot in the door and start a major pipeline down south they would be rolling in money. Especially if they could make the connection for the Northern Lights grass. The rest would sell and more would come. It would be sweet. A nice little earner. But that was a big if. Their profits would double in about a month and they'd be able to purchase a haul twice the amount. It was a couple of keys in cannabis a shit load of Eckies, a load of coke, and a couple of ounce of Heroin, They were sure that it would go smoothly, so they needed to sort out mules.

Pogo and Liam were to go down the back road to Manchester coming out via Carlisle. And Nichol and Giz were going down the highway. And they would meet at a little B and B just in the small town of Prestwich. They would then meet in one of the locals on the edge of Simister. This going well, they would be able to make said journey three maybe four times a year. Depending on supply and demand. Basically if the numbers added up then they would clear overheads like Petrol and overnight stays.

*

Paul still feeling a bit dubious about the whole thing and hoping that his rat hadn't cottoned on to the score. He smiled put down the phone, Banged the kitchen table in delight. He had just lined up the buyers, and knew that Grandad wouldn't fall through, if he did then they were all fucked. It was a couple of days until the deal went down. A lot of money would change hands and also a lot of product. Grandad came round to Paul's and stood waiting at his front door.

Paul answered, "You alright Grandad?"

Leon flashed him a big bright smile and replied, "We on man or are we on man?"

Paul smiled and beckoned Grandad upstairs "Yeah man we is on."

They sat and had a long conversation on what the best way to proceed in the distribution of the payload. The major earner was the smack at a tenner at point two of a gram. It was Angel hair and was really, really good kit. It had quality printed all over it. Anyway Paul gave Grandad an ounce of dope to tide him over. It was dark rocky and had that sweet opium smell about it. It was good shit. They then parted company and just had to wait for the final call, Grandad went to the local phone box and Dialled Pogo, Pogo lifted the receiver, "Awright Gramps?"

Grandad smiled and said "We're on"

*

Day after tomorrow they would be raking it in. It was only two more weeks until school went back. And a boozy drug induced state was on everyone's mind. Everyone was waiting for the score to happen. They were drinking tequila that night and tins of the dark syrupy Gold Beer, which was thick and dark and not to pleasant. But it got you going to where you were going. Grandad had a smile of a man who, has just realised the meaning of life. He was proud as punch and it didn't take much to get him chatting. Danny boy on the other hand was a little dubious about the whole thing.

"Nothing run's that smoothly," He said.

Grandad just beamed some more and replied, "If we get the first shipment without a glitch, Then I'll be happy."

Danny huffed some and said, "You know we got a rat problem?"

Grandad smiled and patted Danny on the neck, "It'll be okay Sully."

Danny was always cautious but this was a shit load of drugs, and Danny was a little paranoid. With good reason, and that reason was the fact that they had tried to open up a network of drugs before and the police had swarmed all over it. But, Grandad had a plan, it was simple, pay the motherfucking police off. This meant they had less, but security, well security was right up to the hilt. Certain desk sergeants were greased up to the max. Fucking Pigs said Grandad then he spat. Grandad had been wondering about a few things how neat and tidy this would be. If they will be taxed by either the police or the local gangs. Things have a way to come back on you, call it fate, call it Karma. But there was a lot of money to be made out of connections, where there is money misery often comes along for the ride. Grandad smiled and thought 'But not all the time'

Chapter 10

Dawn woke that Monday after a fair crack at the task of drinking herself sober, Rose and her had parted company early hours of that Sunday. She made her way to the bus stop. Then waited, there must be some way to contact Grandad even if it meant travelling down south and begging Grandad to at least give her a chance. But fortune favours the few. And she knew she would be graced by his presence, could feel it in her bones. Her heart longed for the guy she was just as surprised as anyone when Rose appeared later that afternoon and said, "I've got you a chance to meet your lover."

She giggled, feeling the excitement bubbling from Rose, "How did your cousin figure out a way we could meet?"

Rose smiled and beckoned her out of earshot. "Well he's got a deal going down soon that needs cut clean."

Dawn smiled at this rolled her eyes and said, "Is it too pure?"

Rose took her hand and continued, "He's been sitting on a stash of narcotics, for about two three months, Just waiting for the right connections. But, and this is a chance at a go with him, He has a half ounce of perfect gear Angel Hair."

She smiled and then said to Rose, "How we going to get in on that action?"

"Well lass, my cousin is a friend of Grandad and has his number." Dawn smiled and continued to listen.

"He has already made contact with him," Dawn groaned and Rose continued "he needs a pharmacist to test the drugs and have cutting agents all-ready in case The smack is too pure"

Dawn smiled, "But how do we get in on the action, and isn't it dangerous."

"Nah it's a pleasure cruise."

Dawn felt warm down on her vagina as if she was about to cum, "ach I'll no get another chance" She smiled at Rose and repeated, "It's no gonna happen again".

Rose went home to phone her cousin and set up some sort of meeting with Grandad and the YBC.

*

Grandad walked back from Paul's house to his Nan's house. He arrived to see his Nan smoking on the little porch.

"Alright Nanna?" He asked then produced a Benson & Hedges pack of Fags.

"Some guy called Andrew called, said he would call tomorrow."

Grandad smiled and lit up his fag. "Och Nan he's a school pal that I protect in the school yard."

She scoffed a small laugh then said, "I don't like people phoning that I haven't met or even know about."

Gramps smiled, "It's all in hand Nan."

Then he pecked her on the cheek, She laughed a little again and finished the conversation, "and young man, I'm not your personal secretary."

He smiled finished has fag then went upstairs to his bed. He would get in contact with Andrew soon as he got up. He fell into a deep stoned slumber.

Chapter 11

Dawn smiled the next morning and stretched. Then went through to the shower and started to wash. Her ample bosom was glistening and erecting her nipples with the warm soapy water, she was very turned on she was a dream of a lassie who was beautiful and dark and also sensuous. She had a little moan to herself as she massaged her pussy letting the hot steam and wet Labia drip beautiful cum onto the shower floor. She washed after she had reached a nice level of stimulation. Then she groaned then came and stood there shaking. Holding one hand on her left breast and the other hand on her clitoris.

She got dressed still buzzing from the climax. She came down the stairs sat down produced a fag, smiled and began to drink her mug of tea. Her mum ruffled her hair and said, "Better than bed head."

Dawn smiled again. "Oh by the way your pal called while you were in the shower. Rose said she had some news that would change your life, Something to do with Manchester."

Dawn smiled at her mum, "Did she say when she would call back?"

Mary smiled at her young Daughter and nodded, My little girl is growing into a fine young woman. She thought. "She said she would phone back after you got back from work."

*

Grandad stayed at home he knew that the phone call from Andy was important. He was getting good vibrations from the night before. Gramps smiled sat down and produced a roll of money. There was a nice roll of at least three grand. But he had already negotiated that money for cutting the angel hair smack. He was just waiting for the phone to go, then he would be in business. He waited a few hours watching the female tennis doubles, It was driving him up the wall. Those little skirts that left nothing to the imagination. The grunting and groaning as they volleyed and returned the ball. '

Fuck I'm horny,' He thought as the match was coming to an end.

The phone rang, it was Andy.

"Awright Andy?" He said gravelly and rough.

Andy smiled and replied, "Aye Grandad how is sunny Manchester?"

Grandad gave a little chuckle and replied, "Better than miserable Edinburgh." Lawson smiled fixed his glasses. "The pharmacist I have procured. Well she knows more about you than I do."

Grandad scoffed and said, "She fit?"

Andy smiled he had seen this coming ages ago. "She's beautiful she has wanted to meet you for years."

Grandad blew a couple of smoke rings. "What stopped her?"

Lawson smiled again and replied, "She's a chemist Leon they get tested and checked vigorously."

Grandad put out his cigarette. "Well we need her for a professional cut job. I'm no getting sent down for killing any smackhead."

Andy laughed, "When have the law ever got their hooks into you?"

Grandad smirked, "Aye well, there is always a first time."

Andy smiled back, "Aye but that'll no be the last time, knowing you".

They said their good byes and Grandad took down the lassies arrival details. A week away at Salford train station. He hung up the phone and went and got himself some Lunch.

*

Pinkie was getting the gist of the score when Shimmy phoned.

"Awright Shimbo?" Asked Pinkie.

"Aye no bad, still a bit buzzed from the other night."

Pinkie started, "You feel that rush? You feel it, it's coming up, we is in the drug trade san."

Shimmey listened intently as Pinkie got down to telling him the details of the score how much part they would play in it. They were muscle and muscle only they didn't get their hands dirty. They were strictly back up. If anything rotten happened they would fill trains and buses and head down to Manchester.

*

Dawn put the phone down and scratched her head. She smiled at her mum and said. "I'm going to Manchester and I'm meeting the love of my life."

Dawns mum hugged her and said, "My wee lass is flying the coop on her way to becoming a young woman."

Dawn hugged her back' "Aye and it's the man of my dreams," She replied.

*

Sully woke that morning with Simone lying next to him, He smiled then started to get dressed. The room smelt of honey and cream. From a good night of passion, they had been all over each other, kissing, hot long kisses and light petting that got heavier and heavier. The more they explored each other the more drenched in soul sweat and groaning. Panting and cum, wet members and glistening wet vibrant bodies. They had each other right where they wanted each other. This was lovemaking of the most passionate sex. Sex. Sex and more sex. Danny put on his tape deck and played 'Step On' By the Happy Mondays.

"I've got to go. Sweetheart" He said as she was putting her hair into a bun, he kissed her lips. Then headed off to Paul's.

His mam shouted as he left, "I suppose I got to feed her as well?"

Sully shouted back, "Yes Mum, thanks Mum" then headed off to Paul's. As he got to the end of his street he saw Grandad lighting a fag and heading in his direction.

"Aye, aye." Said Sully.

Grandad smiled and handed him a fag. "Ach I know you spent the night with Simone," Sully scraped a fag out of Grandads packet and said, "How the fuck do you know?"

Grandad replied, "I can smell her Calvin Klein perfume on you."

Sully laughed and said, "Don't you get points for paying attention."

Grandad smirked and said, "Any way I got this spankassible yum yum coming down from The other side of the bridge. She's a Chemist, and knows exactly what to do about the angel hair smack."

Danny smiled, "You want to do us a favour mate?" He asked Grandad.

"What cuz?" Danny lit up his fag and said. Could you give us a loan of at least fifty" Grandad smiled and said, "What's it fur?"

Danny shrugged his shoulders, "I wanna take Simone to the pictures and then for something to eat. And I mean classy, an Indian meal or a Chinese."

Grandad smiled and peeled of two hundred quid, "Aye nae bother."

They then headed to Paul's and got themselves a half quarter. Each. Grandad smiled as the joint burned and smoke entered his lungs. Not a cough or a wheeze. It was your bog standard three skinner. But boy Grandad packed it and the aromatic soft black gold seal wafted around the room as everyone lit one up.

Paul spoke quietly to Ollie, "Go get the bottle of whisky."

Ollie eyes lit up and he practically flew down the stairs. He came back and stood there with the bottle of Grouse.

Paul Smiled as Grandad noticed the whisky, "Aye Ollie I'll haw a wee dram."

Paul burst out laughing and said, "No mate it's going in the bong."

Grandad grinned and said "Aye well that'll blow oor heeds off"

Paul laughed and said, "Yes mate and seeing as how you are the reason we're celebrating, you get first chug."

Paul began to pour the Whisky in the bong. On the stereo at that time was 'Whiskey in Jar' by Thin Lizzy. Grandad took a big inhale and felt the super-heated whisky mix with the cannabis and melt him to the ground. The rushes were amazing. Paul was next. Then everybody else. It was a very unusual stone that night, very strange as the joints circled and at one-point Grandad and Sully went downstairs and had themselves a set of hot knives each.

Chapter 12

Dawn smiled as she began to pack her things and make sure she had the narcotic test kit that would tell her how pure the gear was. She then stepped out her clothes and into her Jim Jams. Then she began to brush her raven hair, smiling and humming her favourite Doors tune 'Crystal Ship'. She smiled, lay down in her bed and fell into a nice sleep. The next morning she went down the stairs and into the Kitchen. Her mam was, as usual, slaving over a hot stove. But she didn't mind she got pleasure out of being a house mom, She was both happy and content in the kitchen. And her pride and joy was watching her daughter grow into a fine woman.

"You going down to Manchester?" She asked as she poured her darling a nice mug of coffee.

"Aye mam, I've been dying to meet the guy for years."

Her mam smiled and said, "Aye, young love."

She laughed a little at the statement and replied, "Its Grandad of the YBC."

Her mam laughed a little at this and said, "Well first sign of trouble you ditch him and his crew."

Dawn pressed her cheek with her tongue and made a divvy noise. "I know mam," She laid down breakfast and they had a giggle at the expense of Leon.

*

Grandad woke the next morning his mouth dry as a Nun's fanny. He groaned as he pulled his feet off of the bed, his head went thump and began to bang like hell. He put a fag to his lips and went down to the porch to smoke the fag. Nanna was on the porch finishing of a Berkley barge pole of a cigarette. But Leon's Nan preferred them to any of the normal king size.

"Morning young man" she said.

"Shhh Nan, hungover,"

She laughed as he lit up his cigarette.

"You feeling a bit delicate?" She shouted at him.

"Aye Nan calm doon, I'm hungover."

She smiled and walked away chortling at the state of him. She couldn't help but feel a bit superior to him. She got off on it.

Grandad giggled and shout, "Nan too wi coo!" he then put out his fag and went through for a cuppa tea. "I need a favour nan?"

She carried on filling the Kettle, "What and it better be above board?"

Grandad smiled, "I've got this bird coming down for a week or so."

His Nan smiled. "Go on," she continued.

Grandad smiled, "she needs a place to stay." Grandad put two tea bags into the pot and readied the mugs.

"Will she be paying digs?" Asked his Nan.

"How much?" asked Grandad.

"Depends on how long she stays," Grandad smiled as his Nan poured the tea.

"Fifty a night cover it Nan?" She smiled and said, "Where are you getting fifty pounds?"

Grandad smiled and brought out his roll of twenties. "I'll gie ye four nights worth just now."

Leon's Nan got a sudden pang of greed.

"Okay," Grandad peeled off two hundred pound and handed it to his Nan.

She took the money and smiled. "Pleasure doing business with you, youngster. You should really put that in a bank."

Grandad smiled, "Nah Nan this is just change."

His Nanna snorted a laugh, "Just change, he says half a year of pay in notes. And he says it's just change" She took a sip of her mug of tea.

Grandad walked away smiling waving his finger as he left the kitchen. She smiled and looked at the wad of twenties that was on the bunker.

"Thank you indeed," she said as Grandad walked away.

"She'll be here on Saturday," He shouted as he left the porch. And walked round to his cousins house. He had a fair size lump of red seal dope enough for a good few joints.

Danny was smoking out the back of his house, "Awright son?" asked grandad as he got closer to Sully.

"Yes mate" He replied in his thick Mancunian accent. "Got any Vera's?" asked Sully.

Grandad fished around his pockets and came across a packet of Rizla reds. The extra thin rolling papers were a nice smoke leaving a better taste and letting the rich tobacco, and sweet dope time to settle more in your lungs. Grandad smiled and handed the packet to Sully.

"When is your big date with Simone?" asked Grandad.

"Next Saturday," replied Sully.

"Can I come?" asked Gramps.

"Alone?" Said Danny.

Grandad shook his head, "Na man, I got this bird coming doon fae Fife, She's a chemist."

Danny finished rolling his joint, Sparked it up and started to toke. He handed the joint to Gramps. Leon started to puff away on the Joint. Inhale the creamy white skins into his lung's. He beckoned Danny to give him a blow back. Took most of it in, steadied himself for the rush then wow that old familiar rush. From his toes to his head he was stoned Immaculate. The night before being wrecked had just about washed away, until the dope rejuvenated in him sending him to rush central. Danny blew the air out his lungs and said, "Right my turn."

Grandad turned the joint around and breathed on the lit end that was in his mouth. The smoke creamy and pure rushed into Danny's lungs. He stood up and did a spin letting it all into his head. He stopped, holding his breath and said "Yep," then exhaled. Grandad smiled and said, "I always knew you weren't no Bitch ass pussy," he had taken the hit and gained composure. It wasn't rivalry it was well, well it was cool to be this stoned and not to have to think about school. But the nights were drawing in and the Northern Lights score was about to come into fruition. He bent his head back to Scotland, He was having pangs of home sickness. He liked the crew he was with and would always miss them but he had a feeling that he would be able to leave, (When the time was right) and back to merry old Jock land. As it was often called by Paul.

Grandad had nothing to tie him in Manchester. And yes things were going smooth, but in his heart he longed for Edinburgh. He knew this lass that was coming down would be just what he needed. Sully began to walk away and Gramps followed. They got to Paul's house, they took the back way to his house up through a close and round to Paul's door. Paul came down stretching a T-shirt over his head and body.

"Awright lads?" He asked as the two of them went up the stairs.

"Aye," mumbled Grandad.

"Sorted," came the response from Sully. They walked into the bedroom and Sully went straight to the Hi Fi and produced *Final Cut* by Pink Floyd. They let the music play and spaced out accordingly. Rising and dropping with the music mouthing the words at their favourite time, They started to laugh at grandad who was trying to sing with gusto. He thought he was a baritone but when he got too far into the song he would stutter and sit down mumbling "Aye I ken, Am nae Roger Waters." He then would proceed to roll a joint and pass it round sharpish. This was like cause and effect covering the fact that he felt like a twat, an imbecile. But after five minutes of ribbing that he took like a man, the joint would get passed on and the album would draw to its climatic end. See *Final Cuts* got to climatic points in it, both centred around suicide. Thus the final cut. That's what makes it one of the best albums by Pink Floyd.

*

Paul rolled his morning smoke as the rest of them went home. Sully left before Grandad who stayed and rolled a cone with Paul. They toked the fat joint that was the shape of a Cornetto.

Paul smiled and said. "That's what makes you top,"

Grandad smiled and said, "What's that?"

Paul blew some of the hot rocks into his Ashtray, "Your humbleness. Usually Scotsmen are cocky, think they run shit."

Grandad smiled and looked Paul in the eye, "I'll tell yie a secret."

Paul smiled and said, "Go on."

Grandad lay the joint down in the ashtray, "I'm part English."

Paul smiled into Leon's stoned eyes that were half in Egypt half in China.

"No you mean … you mean your British?"

They then fell into a fit of giggles which was full of cheer. It lasted a good twenty minutes. Then the tears rolled from their eyes and they began to gain composure after five more minutes. Grandad stood up swaying like the ocean.

"I got to go home Paul."

Paul smiled and wiped his eyes, surprisingly he was the straighter of the two of them, but that didn't surprise him as Paul was a seasoned dope fiend and Grandad couldn't compete. He could try but it just wasn't going to happen.

Chapter 13

Friday was only a day away. And Grandad was on the phone to Pogo, "You mind the car park at the swimming pool. Aye the fucking commonwealth."

Pogo was about to tell him to stick his fucking deal. But pound signs were flashing in his eyes. He hung up and went through to the sitting room where Vicki was skinning up with her Dope tray. Pogo smiled and began to toke his dope that was Indian soap bar. Liam whistled at Pogo's window.

Pogo opened the window and stuck his head out. "Grandad just rang, we're all go."

Liam smiled and shouted back. "The morrow?"

Pogo threw a sixteenth in a fag packet.

Liam picked it up "Morning bells?" He asked.

"Aye six prompt," said Pogo.

"Aye nae bother" Replied Liam.

*

Dawn was on her last shift for at least a fortnight. She had high hopes, maybe even moving down there. She smiled again as the radio played 'Creep' by Radiohead. She smiled and carried on smoking a cigarette. She was so fucking horny. Her train left Inverkeithing station at 12pm sharp. It would arrive at Salford about 3.15pm. She would meet her lover at said time. She got herself a bottle of vodka and some Red Bull. She mixed it in a water bottle. Half an hour into the journey and she was feeling slightly tipsy. She lit up a fag put on her Walkman and listened to *Pills 'n' Thrills and Bellyaches*. Then after it finished she put on the mighty *Electric Lady Land* by The Jimmie Hendrix Experience. She loved Rainy Day as it cheered her up. It was the kind of song that made you count your blessings. *'Lay back and groove on a rainy Day.'*

*

Grandad got in his taxi at about 2.45pm and sped off to Salford Station. It would take a good twenty minutes to get there, he knew her height eye colour and hair colour. And He knew her accent. He got there and went straight to the platform. Number two. He waited whilst the taxi waited in the car park. Then her train arrived and Grandad knew which carriage she was in, 'G' the smoker's carriage. She stepped of the train with a medium size luggage case with wheels. She also had a satchel with her testing kits and cutting powders. She was wearing comfy New Balance. But she missed her footing after all the red Bull and vodka. Grandad walked over to her and she flung her arms around him and giggled.

"I've been dreaming of you," She put her lips to his left ear and blew hot air in it as she continued, "for-ages."

Grandad Smiled and laughed. They then went to the taxi, she was tipsy all the way. Grandad smiled at the driver, the driver laughed, "She gonna be okay Mate?"

Grandad smiled and handed the driver eighty quid. "Aye pal she's Brand new."

They got back to Prestwich, Gramps thanked the driver who turned and said, "I thought you lot could handle their booze."

Dawn smiled and Grandad held her and walked her to the house. Leon's Nan heard him as he took the lock off the latch.

"Is she here?" came the question, from his Nan.

"Aye she's a bit tipsy though." Grandad replied.

"I'll put the kettle on," said his Nan. She then proceeded to make three mugs of coffee. "She can stay in the double room, and no tom foolery."

Grandad pulled a fag out of his packet and went and stood at the porch and sparked up.

*

Grandad smiled and shouted, "I'm nipping oot to see Danny."

Leon's Nanna shouted okay and Leon went straight to see his cuz. The narcotics should have arrived. And Grandad was eager to see the stash. He got round to Danny's.

"Awright mate?" Came the salutation from Danny.

Gramps had a huge smile on his face. "She a honey like your friend said?"

Gramps shifted his feet and stepped on his fag. Grandad spoke shyly, "Oh she's a peach" Sully Smiled and responded, "Well tell mate."

Grandad smiled and said, "We don't have time, the narcotics are due any time soon," Sully smirked.

*

Liam and Pogo arrived at the local B and B. They sat down at the bar and ordered a couple of pints, while they were waiting to sign their selves into the B and B. Pogo got up and said, "I better make the call to Grandad."

Liam smiled and said, "we had better wait till Nichol and Giz arrive."

Pogo smiled and walked away, "I'm phoning Grandad's connection. No his hoose."

Liam sneered and noticed the place was full of totty. "Aye then we wait."

Pogo followed his gaze and replied, "No that the view is nae good, I mean classy." He said this as his gaze fell onto a beautiful buxom blonde. His eyes followed her as she went into the pool room. "Aye, I mean we are better to wait on Nichol and Giz," he continued.

"Aye I mean we are better to wait for Giz and Nichol," came the reply from Liam.

*

Grandad arrived just as the call was ringing in Paul's house.

Grandad smiled as Paul opened the door, "Is that them?"

Paul "I don't know."

Gregg was in the Kitchen and answered the phone. "Awright lads," came the sombre but in charge Gregg "Is Grandad there?" He cradled the receiver and shouted through to Paul "It's a guy called Pogo, Is Grandad here?"

Paul smiled and shouted back, "Yes mate, he's just arrived." Then the pair of them went through to the kitchen. Grandad took the receiver and spoke to Pogo for about ten minutes. He hung up and said, "They are waiting for my pals to join them."

Paul smiled and said, "Top mate this whole experience has been Top"

Grandad smiled back and said, "Some buzz huh Paul?"

Paul immediately lit up the joint he had made.

Grandad hummed at the whole deal treating it like a quality, posh nosh meal. "Hmmmm."

Then Paul handed him the spliff. "When do we go and collect the product?" asked Paul.

Grandad took a fist blaster, roached the joint and replied, "just got to wait for the other two to appear."

"Which will be in the next hour or two."

*

Dawn was lying in the big double bed semi-conscious and felt very intoxicated, She smiled to herself and said, "Oh boy I'm in it now." She fell asleep.

Grandad was still waiting for the other two to appear.

*

Nichol and Giz had a quick burn. Then headed into the Pub/Bed and B. The first thing they smelt was the ale. The lager and bitter. They sat down at the table that Liam and Pogo had procured. The pair of them were shining on a couple of eckies. Couple of Rhubarb and Custards. Nichol smiled at Pogo and Liam who were totally engrossed in the local talent. Nichol sat down and Giz who was rushing from the charge he took said, "I'll get them in then."

Liam couldn't hold his concentration said, "Aye four Lagers."

Pogo got up and went to the phone and called Grandad. Pogo came back just after Giz put the tray down with the four Fosters.

"He's on his way to us now," Pogo smiled and sipped his lager as he said this. Liam was practically drooling as they sat there waiting on Gramps. They sat back and relaxed, chilled out and drank their amber nectar. Then just as they were about to tan another round. In walked Gramps and Paul. Grandad saw the four of them and walked straight to their table.

"Aye aye lads. Broomie in the toon." He said and they all made wrists with each other, Paul had a joker-toker grin on his face. Pogo shook his handed and slipped him a rhubarb and custard eckie. Pauls grin got wider. Grandad looked at the dealer with a sense of pride. It was cool the product had arrived. And grandad was buzzing on the sheer fact that they had enough product to slice between them.

Grandad smiled and said, "You bring the Angel hair?"

Nichol who was really toasted, "Yeah man we got the kit."

Grandad put his arm on Nichol's shoulder. "Good man, the Northern lights, is that here as well?"

Giz looked at his partner and said, "Aye man chill out."

They went to the van and beat up Ford and gathered the product. Then they got into the car and headed into Paul's. They parked up and went into Paul's with enough product to send them away for at least ten years. But it still felt good. It felt right, everything in its proper place.

Grandad had already paid off the police Two grand to the duty officer. To make sure that all the product got to the various dealers. Then a ten per cent of profits to the local DS This would be made every month or so depending on how the drugs flowed.

Grandad smiled and said to Paul. "I have arranged for a Chemist with a testing kit and cutting agents. She arrived today."

Paul smiled and replied, "Is she a honey?"

Grandad smirked and said, "Aye she's nae bad."

Paul whistled a small bomber and said, "You'll be taking all our jobs and homes. It's like we are being invaded from Jock land."

Grandad lit up a fag then he clapped his hands and said, "Aye we sort the product tomorrow then Danny and me and wee Dawn, and Simone, we are all going to see a movie then for a Chinese."

Paul hugged himself whilst he got a rush from the Eckie. Grandad checked the stash and after he was satisfied that it was all there he left. He had some explaining to do with his Nan.

Chapter 14

Shimmey went home and on the way home he stopped at a phone and dialled the B and B that Liam, Pogo and Giz and Nichol were at. The receptionist listened as Shimmey spoke with his broad, thick accent; "Is my mates in the hotel?" Gary Williamson. Liam Burnette and Craig Nichol. And Barry Baxter?"

The receptionist put the music on whilst she checked if there keys were gone. "Yes sir, they are in."

Shimmey relaxed, all he kept thinking was blue lights and the four of them in Strangeways Prison.

"Awright, Shimbo?" Came the voice of Giz. "Aye we made it."

Shimmey sighed with relief and said, "Thank fuck, You know your mother will hae kittens if you dinea phone her."

Giz looked around making sure nobody could hear him. "Sam broon, sam broon. I'll phone her soon as we finish."

Shimmey, sneered and snorted then said, "Aye well yae better."

Shimmey spat and then hung up the phone. "Fuckers, they should have sent me wae Giz."

He had a fucking better sense than anyone when it came to product. He wouldn't have waited until the last minute to test and cut the smack. He felt around the change drawer, but nothing. He walked home smoking a doobie. "Grandad you jammy fucker!" he said as he neared the stairwell where Grandad's mam lived. Shimmey stayed just a short jaunt up the hill from Grandads house.

*

Pinkie smiled a huge smile, lay on his bed smoked a fag and smiled some more. His mum had fixed him up with a lass called Pauline. It was the last half year of school for him. How he had managed to get a result in Physics was a complete guess to him and everyone else. But this Lass was class, beautiful, bubbly and blonde. Pinkie fell into a narcotic filled sleep. Woke the next morning and had no hangover. He was beyond hangovers, he was in love. He stretched into his 501's and then put his feet into a pair of timbies. He then put on his shirt that he had got from Next. He stood at the mirror to fix a slick back hairdo. He looked into his own eyes and said, "The killer awoke before Dawn."

He smiled then went and got himself some breakfast. "You tell your wee brother to phone his mam,"

Pinkie started to tuck into his breakfast, "Aye Da," he said. "And tell your pals I want him home safe by Monday." Pinkie smiled a viperish smile and said, "Aye Da."

"Leave him alone," came the dulcet tone of his mam. "He's gearing up to meet his new lover."

Pinkie smiled knowing and thinking, 'They'll no ruffle my hair with all that gel on it. I hope'. Pinkie got up from the table and pushed a bit of toast in to his mouth, "Right Mam I' away to meet Pauline."

She smiled. "Mind and get yur wee brother tae phone?"

Pinkie put on his river island leather coat and went to catch the bus to Moredun. Pinkie was looking forward to the meeting. Her family weren't well off but they had money. James had fallen for her the instant they looked at each other. It was love at first sight. She had pink vibrant lips and long blonde hair. Tall, well she was a couple of inches beneath Pinkie. But this didn't matter as well as the saying goes we are all the same size in bed. Best things come in small packages. He got off the bus and headed straight to Pauline's house. He rapt on the door and Pauline answered.

"Hiya Doll," said Pinkie.

She smiled and waved him on through to the sitting room where her mother and sister sat having a chin wag and a cup of Bruce Lee. Her sister was beautiful and her mum was no too bad either. The three of them were stunning blondes. Pinkie smiled and said, "Good afternoon ladies"

The mother and daughter smiled and went off in unison. "Hi Pinkie."

Pinkie smiled and went and sat down.

Pauline made her way to the Kitchen. "Want a cold one Pinkie?" she asked.

Pinkie smirked "If it's Becks, Then definitely, yes."

She smiled and went to the fridge "Yep you're in luck James I got two left."

Pinkie smiled and winked as he took of the top of the bottle with his teeth.

"Cheers sweetie" he said then took a swig of the German beer. He relaxed and had a nice beer rush. "It's okay if I stay a night right?" Pauline's mum smiled and said, "Yes of course you can, And my name is Susan."

James Smiled and thought 'What a darling' 'What a bunch of darling's' The three of them beautiful bouncing bombshell blondes. Oh tonight was going to be dynamite. As the night continued Pinkie almost forgot. He fished out the piece of paper he had with the B and B that his brother and Nichol were staying.

"Can I use your Phone?" Susan smiled and said, "course you can".

He breathed a sigh of relief and said, "Thanks."

He then got taken into the next room that was obviously a dining room. He picked up the phone and dialled the B and B's number. It rang for a minute or two.

"Prestwich Arms, can I help you?" Came the question from the obvious female. "I'd like to find out as the whereabouts of a party of four." The receptionist smiled and responded "Names Please?"

Pinkie Smiled and said "Nichol, Burnett, Williamson and Baxter."

She smiled "Arrived yesterday. Checking out the day after tomorrow."

Pinkie smiled as Pauline sidled past. Then the receptionist carried on "They aren't in the bar at the moment. Do you want to leave a message?"

Pinkie smiled and said. "Please if isnea any trouble."

The receptionist reached for a pen and paper. "Okay sir, who is calling?" "It's James Williamson. Gary Williamsons brother"

The receptionist then continued, "And what is the message?"

Pinkie Smiled, "Your mother wants to know where you are?" He finished the conversation and hung up.

*

Meanwhile Dawn was sleeping off her drunkenness. She smiled and got up and headed down the stairs. How long had she waited for this opportunity. How long had she fantasized about her and Grandad. Now it was real.

"Hi Mrs Gratton."

Leon's Nan scoffed at this and said with a little chuckle, "Sheila call me Sheila."

Dawn smiled as she sipped her sweet tea, "Thank you Sheila."

Gramps wandered home nursing a hangover with some Irn Bru and a smoke. He got to the porch where his Nan and Dawn were stood having a fag and some gentle conversation. Grandad smiled and stood on his fag end.

"Awright ladies?"

And the two of them giggled and said, "We're in better shape than you."

Grandad smirked, "Aye that it might be."

Dawn blew smoke and carried on. "Where are we going the night?"

Gramps smiled. "We're going to see a Movie then we are going for a Chinese." Dawn smiled and uttered under her breath, "You smoothie you."

He smiled at the young lady and said, "you Willnae need to put your hand in your pocket. Whose for a brew?" asked Leons Nan.

Dawn smiled and extinguished her fag. "Aye Sheila that sounds Braw."

The three Spraffed till after lunch. Then Dawn and Grandad headed off to Paul's. Danny was sat in the living room of Paul's house. With the four mad jocks. Paul was peeking on an acid. And the rest were skinning up. The music on the hi fi was The Doors 'Waiting for the Sun'. *'Hello, Hello. I need my Baby Yeah'* That song was blasting through the house and Paul was gleaming, The Acid was a double dipped Strawberry and a good one at that.

Grandad Knocked gently on the door. And Gregg Answered.

"It's Scotty." He said then ushered Dawn and Grandad through to the front room. Grandad took a quick look at Paul who was tripping out his nut. Grandad nodded his head and gave a quick chuckle.

"How long has Paul been peaking?"

Gregg laughed and put his arm around Gramps shoulder, "About an hour," he said. "Is there any more?"

Gregg shrugged and replied, "No until later."

Danny stood up and walked up to Grandad, "Awright Cuz?" Grandad smiled as at the same time he was handed a joint and a Becks.

"Aye no bad," replied grandad. "We'll get the business over wie and then we'll go oot"

Sully smiled and took a toke on his joint. Dawn stood there at the doorway waiting for her click. Grandad took the parcels upstairs and nodded for Dawn to follow him up the stairs. She had a large satchel with testing kits and powder to cut the Heroin. She smiled at Grandad and said, "Can I get a drink?" Gramps smiled and went over to a small cooler and produced a bottle of diamond white. He popped the cap and handed it to her. She smiled as she took a swig of the cider and smiled and said "Thanks."

Then she began to test the Angel hair, making sure that it was what it was.

"Yep the ph balance is right. It's pure, how much do you want to cut it?"

Paul who had come up the stairs, because he was tripping and wanted to see this young pharmacist set up with a paraffin lamp, And mineral water. Then when she had tested the smack. She took enough for a burn and enough for a pin. Paul came right into the room with a bottle of lemon. He fixed the pin and Olley took the shot after letting the pin cool for a minute or two. Then he smacked his bitch up letting the smooth rush of Heroin pulse through his body. Olley smiled as he turned Chinese on them.

"Oh that's good shit," he said and let the rushes do their work.

*

Dawn smiled and took a comfort drag of a joint. "Yep it was pure but I gave it whack of whitening. Enough to cut it in two."

Grandad swigged on his Becks and Indian toked his joint until it was roached. He was high as the almighty. "That's Great Dawn we got the cinema to go to so tidy up and get ready."

Grandad smiled at the Four grand that would soon be eight grand. Give it a couple of weeks and that would double again. Then they would have a safe connection to the south from the north. He smiled a nice grin Then carried on ushering Dawn and her kit out of Paul's and back to his Nan's were he would get changed and then the four of them would head into town. They were planning on seeing a Brad Pitt movie *Seven* with Morgan Freeman. They met up with Danny and jumped into a taxi then went to the Bury Cinema and watched what Grandad thought was Brad Pitts best movie.

They sat through the whole thing and found they're nerves jangling at the end of the movie. They then went to a local Chinese restaurant and had a lovely slap up feast. Grandad had an itch in him, it was the state Paul was in he hadn't taken a trip in ages, and knew that they were one of the best trips around. He smiled at Dawn who was quick to suss what was going on in the head of Leon. She pushed a small match box into Leon's hand. Gramps went outside and opened up the matchbox. It had three double dipped acid Jaggers lips. These were also a quality acid that was around then.

He took one and looked at Sully and Simone. "Should I get them to split one?"

Dawn smiled and replied, "Gie them one each, I peaked ages ago."

Grandad smiled and said Okay, then handed Sully the matchbox and said, "There's one each, for you and Simone."

Sully and Simone dropped their tabs. But the drawback with that acid was it took ages to gleam. But when it did it was a beautiful rush and worth the wait. Grandad wasn't much of a smack head. He was a rush trippy kinda guy. But then it's different strokes for different folks. He smiled as they got in the taxi. His trip was just building up. The food the wine, the good company. It was the best rush he had in ages. Dawn cradled into Grandads arm as Sully and Simone got out the taxi and headed to his house. They arrived at Grandad's, nanna's house. And Grandad paid the guy and gave him a good tip. He walked Dawn to his front door, He opened the door with his key. Then the two of them headed to her bed. They lay kissing and spooning each other. Getting riled up then caressing each other, mutual masturbation. Then They started to explore each other. Sucking, rubbing, getting each other hard and wet. This went on most of the night, then after several climaxes they stopped for some vodka and cola and some party powder. (Cocaine).

*

Dawn awoke early afternoon, it was Sunday. And Sheila was cooking eggs and bacon. Leon opened his eyes and was immediately overpowered by the morning breakfast smell. He slipped into a pair of Sonetti. Jeans and donned a Fila sweatshirt. Dawn slid into a skirt and put on a light cardigan from Next. Grandad smiled as he took the plate with two rolls with egg and bacon. He put a splash of Daddies red sauce, you know the sour one. Then wolfed them down. Dawn did likewise.

"You were late in last night."

Grandad smiled and took a swig of sweet baby tea.

"What film did you go and see?"

Grandad went, "It was a tense and taught thriller with Brad Pitt and Morgan Freeman."

Sheila asked with enthusiasm, "What was it like?"

Grandad smiled as did Dawn. Grandad started to recount some but not too much of the film.

"Sounds interesting," She said and Dawn smiled and went to the porch to have a cigarette.

Sheila was engrossed in his retelling of the movie, He gave brief description but managed to leave the bones of the film covered. He finished and said, "You have to see the rest to believe the rest." He joined Dawn on the Porch and had a cigarette.

Pinkie smiled and exited the bedroom and went to the loo. His head was pounding from the dehydration of a hangover (His own fucking fault) But he smiled as it was a glorious Sunday birds were singing and the sun was out in Moredun. He went back into the room and put on his Armani top and Lee Jeans. Pauline smiled "Everything okay?" He smiled and responded with a gentle kiss to her wrist, knowing how such a small gesture, whilst remaining soft and delicate meant to his sweet heart. Yeah he was in love. For the very first time he went over to the hi fi and put on UB40, *'Wise man say only fools rush in'.* the song was perfect fit for the mood and lifted his heart. He smiled and took a draw of his cigarette. "I need to go sweetheart."

She gave a feminine groan, small and gentle. Pinkie smiled at this she wasn't displeased this was just her teasing him gently. He loved her his feelings were strong.

"I gotta go honey," Pinkie said as he zipped up his two hundred pound leather Jacket, that came from River Island. He was wearing his Kickers shoes and looked at his Timberland watch. "I need to contact Gizmo."

He then left and got on a bus. Back to Sighthill.

Chapter 15

Shimmey counted his tick list. Yep it was all there, three hundred sobs. He rounded the corner just as the bus stopped and saw Pinkie getting off.

Shimmey shouted to Pinkie, "Pinkie Its me."

James coughed a little and produced a twenty deck of Regal Fags. He lit one and handed one to Shimmey. "You better go and square off that debt with Biscuit."

Shimmey smiled. "Aye, aye I think I better"

They stood and chewed over the recent going on's. Then they parted company.

"Come by later we'll hae a spraf and laugh."

Shimmey shook Pinkies hand and said as they parted. "Aye man I'll be there, I'll be there just got to pay the main man."

"You need anything exotic whilst I'm there?" Pinkie smiled and said, "a couple of dancing sweeties would be nice."

Shimmey smiled, "Coming right up." Then off he went.

He smiled at the fact that he had been introduced a couple of years ago by Leon and one of his classmates. Said classmate was also responsible for Leon's Nickname, Grandad. The boy's name was Daz Duke. And he was fond of teasing Leon. Grandad's reputation had only grew, the more he hung around doing dope and being a degenerate. Anyway, Shimmey crossed the underpath and headed towards the flats. He got up the stairs the walked across the balcony to Biscuits door and knocked. First thing he heard was Biscuits rottweiler barking.

"Who is it?" came a gruff voice from inside the flat.

"It's me Shimmey."

Biscuits dog barked some more, then quieted as Biscuit called him to heel. "Satan shut up."

The door opened then a waft of dope hit Shimmey's nostrils. All Shimmey could think was Shan grilla. Biscuit who was well built and ruggedly handsome with his blonde hair. He was wearing his working gear that was dusty as he was a joiner to trade. He worked for Beaties the Construction and Demolishing company.

Shimmey followed Biscuit who asked him to, "Sit doon man."

Shimmey sat down and produced The money for his trade, Biscuit counted it and said, "Is there anything else you need?"

Shimmey smiled and replied, "Yeah a gram of coke and six eckies."

Biscuit smiled at him and said, "How's things going down south?"

Shimmey smiled back and replied, "It's going great."

Biscuit gave a little laugh, "Aye Grandad knows how to do the business."

Shimmey smiled and took out a fag and lit up. "You make sure he comes to see me when he gets back."

Shimmey blew a smoke ring, smiled and responded, "Aye Biscuit Aye."

Biscuit then went and got his brass scales out and weighed out a gram of coke and gave Shimmey six eckies. They were Mitsubishis. A quality Eckie.

Shimmey smiled, "That will do just nicely." He said and produced one hundred and ten pounds. Sixty for the E's and fifty for the white. He smiled as Biscuit weighed out the rock.

"Anything else?" He asked with a smile on his face.

Shimmey flicked his smoke into the ashtray, "Nah man that's sweet enough." They shook hands then shimmey left.

*

Grandad and Dawn went round to Pauls house. The party had long since finished and Paul was tidying up he still had the Joker smoker grin in his eyes.

Grandad smiled at him, "How you daen?"

Paul smiled and said, "Sound mate."

Grandad laughed and replied, "Still buzzing huh?"

The question hit Paul and made him smile that little bit more. "The product get moved safe enough?"

Paul emptied an ashtray into a black bin bag. Dawn sat down, "alright love was last night good enough?"

Dawn smiled and replied, "Aye man, It was a cool film."

Paul carried on cleaning the house. "Yes Mate the product was safely cut and moved."

Grandad smiled and replied, "My boys, did they cause any trouble?"

Paul shook his head, "No it was a cool little party." Paul sat down for a minute and asked, "When do they go back?"

Grandad snorted, "The day after tomorrow."

Paul smiled through his eyeballs. "I suppose we better make tonight legendary."

Grandad smiled, sat down and began to build a joint. He rubbed the hash between his fingers and dusted it over the cigarette. That was a clean build. He finished licking the skins and smiled then lit it up. It was a smooth piece of dope, rocky. And sweet scented. Dawn smiled and looked at Paul. "Got any tin foil?"

Paul shrugged and said, "Yeah doll I got some," Having the sense to keep himself steady continued. "You got enough for me to have one to." Dawn smiled her wee pearly teeth out, she always scored when she was testing and cutting. This was called Dragon rights. She handed over a small piece of skin with point two of a gram in it. "Aye of course I take a small amount wae me as well as money for the service."

Paul's smile was growing bigger and bigger. He sat down with the skag then built himself a tooter as did Dawn. They then both of them began to chase the dragon. The two of them pro's in the game. Grandad smiled as the two of them got on like a house on fire. They spraffed as they chased their beetles along the foil. Grandad carried on toking his joint. An hour later they were blessed with the rest of the YBC, Liam, Giz, Baxter and Nichol. Who had enough product on them to orbit Arnie. The rest was gone man I mean gone. Sold with a healthy Profit. They had hooked up with some boys from Leeds. And were left with a tonne of cash and some product that was cut and would make a tidy profit. The Angel hair lasted what, about two hours. That done, the rest of the product was sold that very same evening. Paul and Dawn were smoking joints and talking business, he was quite pleased with himself. He had managed to hold the whole process together. And also made himself a profit.

"So how long you known Grandad?" He asked as the Jimi Hendrix blasted through the house. "Oh I've known Grandad for years now." Paul nodded. "We call him Scotty round here."

Dawn smiled and sipped her bottle of Diamond white, and replied, "Oh I bet he cherishes that nickname." Paul sat back down for a second and asked. "How did he get the nickname Grandad?"

Dawn laughed and answered. "One of his crew called him it. Something to do with the eczema and it leaving him looking older."

Paul smiled and went "Oh so it started as in class insult and Grandad just went along with it"

Dawn smiled, "Yep" She answered.

"You know the girls are all daft about him here."

She smiled, "Yeah I know."

Grandad was talking to Giz and Nichol. Giz was smiling whilst drinking and toking. Grandad cupped his neck and said, "Ok Giz did you phone your mother?"

Giz sat down and took a toke and a pull of his bottle. "Fuck I knew something was missing."

Grandad looked at him and said, "Well you better get downstairs and phone her."

It was nine o-clock and Mrs Williamson would heading away to bed. Giz smiled and let the phone ring, then all of a sudden it was answered but not by his mum no it was his Da. He gulped as his father answered, "Williamson residence can I help you?"

Giz bit the bullet, "Awright Da?" Came the question.

"Aye son I'm daen Grand, where the hell are you and what's that racket?"

Giz now had opportunity to shit himself and dive in. "I'm at a club Da," he said nervously.

"Aye well when you coming hame?" Giz smiled as his pants told a dark tale. "Day after tomorrow," replied Giz.

"Good and dinea be ringing here after eight again," Gizmo smiled and replied. "Aye Da". Then he hung up.

*

Grandad Looked at Dawn just as she finished the conversation she was having with Paul. It was coming on midnight and Gramps was getting horny.

"You right doll?" He asked and helped her into her Next Jacket, it was a tweed and then he wrapped the scarf around her and he pulled his green and cream Sonetti reversible jacket on. Paul smiled and handed a wrap of speed and a couple tabs of acid. Then he went over to his drawer and pulled a freshly chopped ounce of rocky dope.

"This is on the house," he then sparked up a doobie and waved the pair of them goodbye. Gregg smiled as the two of the sidled by, "Good luck Scotty," He said.

Grandad smiled and took a kiss on the cheek from Dawn. Simone and Sully were having a good all you can eat kissing session. Grandad chuckled and said as he crossed over to the door "Danny Boy the pipes the pipes are calling."

Danny waved him whilst still kissing Simone. Grandad smiled through his eyes and wondered whether this was all too real. They then headed back to Parrenthorn Road, to his Nanna's. Grandad had this sly cowboy walk like he was dragging his right leg as if he had a revolver. But what he had on him was half a pool cue. That slipped into his pocket. But he only went tooled when business was being conducted. Tonight he was armed. But nothing had popped off. Nothing heavy duty had happened. He went into the kitchen and opened the freezer and produced a nearly full bottle of Absolut vanilla vodka and two large bottles of Vanilla coca cola. Dawn got hold of two tumblers and they retired to the guest bedroom of Che' la Gratton. They started with a gentle roll around on the covers. Kissing and fondling each other. They had a light petting session. And smiled into each-other's eyes. The drugs, the alcohol fuelling their lust and breathing each other in. Hot burst of air as they breathed in. The throbbing, the heartfelt desire as they started to remove each other's clothes, gently, passionately. But taking their time with each other. Grandad fell to his knees with his head between her legs. He could smell her honey dark, aromatic juices. Her tight Pepe jeans were the only thing stopping him drowning in her ether. He carried on breathing her in whilst massaging her vagina under her jeans. Then snap the button came away. Then calmly he took down her Jeans. She was wearing a pair of black lace knickers. He turned her round gently and his cock, which was just as wet as her peach, penetrated her the two of them having a nice sexual rush. He smiled as they both started to moan and relax into a comfortable screwing position. Then they carried on sucking spooning and mutual masturbation. She loved him and loved him good. She had been patient and had got her man. The session of sex lasted what felt like a life time was in fact four hours. They eventually fell asleep cuddling each other and relaxing. The night moved on and Gramps was in heaven.

*

He woke the next morning, though it was closer to mid-day, sat up and listened. No, something was wrong, it was too quiet, He put on his Ted Baker top and pushed his blade down the back of his trousers.

"Nan," he shouted as he headed towards the stairs.

His Nana was holding a heated discussion with a couple of stiffs. Gramps got to the door and one of them lunged at him.

"Come here you junky lanky piece of shit?"

Grandad who was just waiting for the local vigilantes, as he had heard had been the cause of most of the drug busts, there were all kind of rumours about these guys, some say they were just working the area for their own personal gain. Others said that one of them had lost a son to smack and was very bitter about.

Grandad looked the guy dead in the eye, "You want you're square go's dea yae?"

Grandad reached for his blade and Dawn caught the sinister steely look of Grandad as he began to approach the guy who was at least twice the age of Grandad. He kept snarling and said through hissing teeth, "Aye I want my goes you Scottish pansie."

Grandad swiped his blade across the guys arm. It was razor sharp and burst the man like a ripe tomato. But the wound was a serious one, and Gramps knew it. The guy carried on coming and Dawn and his Nan got out the way. Grandad produced his half a pool cue. And slammed the thing in the fucking guys face smashing his teeth and breaking his jaw. The other guy put both his hands in the air.

"I'm no wanting trouble pal, just let me pick my mate up and get out of here."

Grandad growled a smashing Sicilian scowl. He looked at the two pieces of shit and said, "Fucking next time I finish the job."

The guy was pumping blood as he got to the blue piece of shit Sierra. Grandad sat down and lit up a fag. Coughed and regained composure.

"What's for breakfast Nan"

She chortled and said Bacon and eggs. Dawn smiled, her eyes widened to what sort of a man he was, and yes it was a turn on. Grandad was a strange one. He was a wild one, he was tough and that meant a lot to some. This gang of vigilantes, had made his day. He smoked some more then said as Dawn handed him a bacon and egg roll, "Cheers doll." He wolfed into it. He was going to have to mention it to Paul but it could wait.

The polis would be next, "Oh the fucking joys" He swore and finished of his bacon and egg roll. Grandad got up and poured himself some sweet tea. And phoned Ian Polland his mate to get round and get round sharpish. He then went and gathered up the Narcotics and stuffed them into the bag he had procured from his Nan. Polland arrived and Grandad shoved the bag with all the drugs into Polland's face.

"Where am I taking them?"

Grandad growled some more and said, "It's the thing you fear the most."

Polland smiled as Grandad said, "Half tae Breenies, and half to Reno." Polland smiled at him, "hedging your bets mate, wise decision."

Grandad smiled and said, "Aye so move."

Polland vanished down the tunnel at the end of the street.

*

James walked back from the centre of the toon, and headed towards his house. He had been in touch with his brother who was about to head home a day early as the Polis were about to descend on them They helped clean the house then scarpered, a quick jaunt to pay the owner of the hotel. Then like a flash gone two separate ways. One the highway the other the back roads, both holding but neither of them were risking an under the influence charge. They would both meet back at Pinkies between seven and eight o clock.

Grandad smiled at Dawn. Who was smiling at him. "I take it you want to Head back up the road tae?" Dawn grabbed his arm and wrapped it around her "With all this going on no siree I just watched you give someone which I can only call The treatment."

He smiled and said, "Well when they come, you tell them that you were testing eckies for the local man, and that you had hired me for back-up." Grandad looked deep into her eyes then went cockeyed then straightened them again. Dawn laughed and Grandad gave her a kiss on the cheek and said. "Thank you doll most women would have run a mile seeing me get messy."

Dawn smiled and responded "I please to aim"

*

Pinkie sat on his doorstep smoking a fag and re relating what had just happened. Shimmey and him had been planning a nice night out with the intentions of getting totally shit faced, Pinkie started on his third lager. He was nice and toasted with the three eckies. They were giving the night a nice buzz. And he had his eye on a girl sat in the corner. But common senses was telling him

'Nah, nah, nah' and Pauline was on his mind. He smiled as Shimmey sat down with a jug of sex on the beach.

"Aye aye," He smiled, "She's giving you the glad eye."

Pinkie smiled sipped his lager and answered, "Nah man I'm spoken for."

Shimmey scoffed and replied, "wouldnea stop me."

Pinkie laughed and said, "Aye well go ahead."

Shimmey stood up, straightened himself out then headed towards the lassie.

"If you score, mind and leave me half that gram of cocaine."

Shimmey reached into his pocket and fished out the plastic baggie. "Hae it all" then handed the gram to Pinkie. Then he walked over to the lassie. Pinkie smiled at himself. And carried on with his lager. The music was pumping Techno. The DJ was Carl Cox. Pinkie smiled and decided to head to the toilet to have a bump of coke. He took a line and felt the rush instantly.

"Sweet Jesus that's quality," he said as the rush hit him. Then as he was just about to leave. A tall dark haired guy walked in, "That your mate?"

Pinkie twisted up his face and replied, "Excuse me."

The guy had a bug up his arse. And to top it off he was English. And obviously gunning for a fight. Pinkie growled to himself. This was trouble and it was trouble he didnea need.

"Who do you fight for?" asked Pinkie.

The guy stood right by the door, and stopped all kinds of escape. The guy smiled, Pinkie felt around his jacket for his kosh and scalpel. The guy produced a lock back, big as fuck blade.

"My name's Ron and you're getting Tanned."

Pinkie produced his Kosh, then took out his surgeon sharpened scalpel.

"Well I'm Pinkie of the YBC."

Then the two them got down to it. Pinkie was furious and fast as he swiped with his Kosh. Then followed through with his scalpel. Slicing the guy just below his bottom lip. The guy grimaced and tried to plunge Pinkie with his lock back blade. But Pinkie saw it coming and swung his kosh hard onto the guys knife hand. He heard then saw the guy drop his blade his hand obviously broken. Pinkie stepped forward and asked as he pushed the scalpel under the Casuals chin, "I asked you a question, what fucking crew do you fight for?"

The guy knew he was beat. "Leeds," he muttered. Pinkie gave him a good kick to his bollocks and exited the toilet. He walked right up to Shimmey.

"Come on she's no alone," Shimmey stood up and started to complain. But Pinkie was having none of it "A fucking Leeds boy. I just went toe tae toe wae a Leeds boy."

Shimmey looked at Pinkies hands that were covered in blood. "Oh you just did the damage to a Leeds boy." Pinkie Snarled and said, "Aye and you know he'll be right onto his crew and we'll be at war" Shimmey stuck out his hand a whistled for a taxi. The two of them got out of Dodge.

*

Grandad smiled as he saw the Polis drive next to his Nan's house. The two gentlemen exited there car and headed down the drive way. They were armed to the teeth, with mace and Chinese tonfa shaped truncheons.

Grandad smiled lit up and said, "Afternoon gentlemen how can I help you on this fine day?"

The two police men looked at the spray of blood that was leading out into the garden.

"You mind telling us what happened son?"

Grandad made the story thick, and juicy saying how the two men had tried to grab his Nan and being as he was the only man in the house, he had to fend them off with a weapon he had, what as he could only call a sin to have to use. It was after all his best pool cue. Two police men took statements and left it at this. If anything were ever to happen again they were not to deal with the situation themselves and they were to call the police.

Dawn went back upstairs and got her fags. Grandad smiled as his aunt Carol came down the drive way.

"Young man, young man." She said then pulled him close and gave him a peck on the cheek.

His Nana smiled. "You should have seen it," continued Leon's Nan. "I mean I knew my Grandsons could handle themselves but him he was a proper soldier. Gratton fighting spirit."

Carol smiled as Dawn came down the stairs. "And you'll be the young lady that's been dotting on my nephew?" She smiled and then took her hand on this business like day.

Dawn smiled and said, "Charmed."

Carol smiled and said, "It would seem so".

Grandad put the kettle on. And brewed up some fine Tetley tea. Whilst the kettle boiled. The three ladies got to gabbing over current affairs. Grandad stood in the side doorway having a joint. He began to chill out as the tea was served, he smiled this had turned out to be a no bad jaunt down here. Dawn was firing on all cylinders.

Spraffing, laughing gabbing about differences, politics and Carol was taken with her, as she left she pointed at her and mouthed the words, 'She's a keeper.' Then she headed home.

Chapter 16

Leon's Aunt Gill was first to phone Carol and get the juicy gossip. Carol spilled the beans on all the action that had taken place and how cute as a wee button Leon's new girl was. Gill and Carol spent the better part of three hours talking.

Grandad and Dawn had a nice meal with Leon's Nan then headed back round to Paul's. Paul was in the toilet shooting up a small pin. Grandad strode up the stairs and heard Sully and Simone kicking it tight. They were laughing and giggling as Paul shot himself to Palookaville. Grandad walked into the room and made a wrist with Sully.

"My fucking main man," said Sully.

Dawn and Simone started to talk whilst they had a couple lines of speed. Grandad sat down and built a joint. The house was about to go into full swing. Grandad put some Oasis on but that didn't last long as someone wanted to play Thin Lizzy. The one that got everybody was 'Whiskey in the Jar'. Then a number of bongs were lit up and you could hear the party away up in Simister. That was a good half a mile away. Grandad caught Paul on his way to get another beer, Gramps asked him if he had any Yogurts.

Paul smiled at him and said, "Yes mate."

Grandad shouted up into the bedroom, "Sully, Yoda pronto."

Sully flew downstairs. Danny looked at Paul as if to say "Huh." Paul went, "You know where the kitchen is." Danny walked through to the kitchen and produced a fair size of a lump. Four, five joints worth. They put a little knob of butter onto a spoon each and melted the dope then when they had finished cooking the dope they plunged it into the yogurts and smiled as it hissed into the crème la crème.

Paul came through and spoke quietly to Gramps, "Scotty my man. The passing trade alone has sorted out three or four times the profit."

Grandad shrugged as the dopey Yoda took effect. "Aye Paul to sinners and winners and having a good time."

Grandad sat down and again built a spliff. The song that was on was 'Jailbreak' by Thin Lizzy. *'Tonight there's gonna be a jailbreak so don't hang about the town.'* Then the song moved on to 'Chinatown'. *'Living and dying down in China Town you'll be living or dying down in Chinatown'.*

Dawn sat next Grandad and had a burn. "I need to go hame darling."

Grandad smiled, "When darling, when?"

She smiled as she put her arms around him, "two more days."

"Och darling that's ages away," Replied Gramps. Next thing they were back into Leon's Nans house. The petting heavy as if they had waited a year to get that close.

*

Pinkie wusnea daft what he had just done was well, lit was a big no-no. He had left the guy in pieces. Gripping his bollocks as if he had just been kicked by a mule.

And a broken arm and slice right off the top. Yep this would nea lie right with the Leeds Mob. No they would want an example at least that or a meet. Pinkie relaxed a little as he got round tae Leg's hoose. He buzzed up then waited.

"Awright Who is this?"

Pinkie smiled and replied, "it's me Pinkie." Pinkie smiled and waited for the door to be let off its magnetic seal. It buzzed and Pinkie went on up. The door opened and the fog spilled out.

"Awright Pinkie?" Said a voice at the back of the room. He was handed a joint of o' Raymie and Cha took a big hit from a bong. Cha spoke as the smoke was passed out his lungs.

"Aye Pinkie. We ken what happened last night."

Pinkie toked his Spliff, "Leeds boy, Aye someone tried to chew Biscuits Balls off over the phone. Demanding that you and your pal were served up bollocks first."

Cha laughed, "Biscuit was just as charming back. He waited until the yappy wee dug stopped yapping down his ear Then said in his best and blessed tone. "Fuck you, fuck Leeds and fuck everyone in England. That's all part of the service. So sweetheart you come and you come alone. You will get the message. Then everybody in the house started to bark and howl. YBC, YBC the fucker hung up and Biscuit is proud of you."

Pinkie smiled and sat down.

"Thought I was for the concrete foundations for sure."

Cha smiled handed him the bong whilst Cyprus Hill were playing in the back ground 'Hits from the Bong Hits from the Bong'. Pinkie just realised that Grandad was in Bandit Country. So he stood up and squatted next to Cha.

"What aboot Grandad?" Cha smiled and sank a tin o' lager.

"Aye what aboot him?" He then gave a small laugh. "He's no in any danger. Well I better get in contact wae him anyway."

Pinkie looked at Legs and said, "Can I use your Phone?"

Legs smiled. Then the buzzer went. It was Liam, Nichol, Giz and Baxter. Legs stuck his head oot the window and clocked the four o them. "Awright boys?" Then he went back inside and buzzed them up.

Giz saw his brother was there "How's it goin Pinkie?"

Pinkie stopped and let the question sink in. "How's it goin, how's it goin" He muttered under his breath. "Well now I got bad news and I got bad news." He sniffed and continue, "You want it in ascending order?"

Giz looked at him with a curious eye, "Sorry I fucking asked."

Pinkie sighed, "well you want to know how it's going, still interested?"

Legs got hold of the two of them and asked the ten million pound question, "is it fanny central or queerdo weirdo country?" Giz responded and responded well. "Fanny central"

Nichol smiled and said, "and they love their disco Biscuits. Now how's everything going?"

"Well," replied Pinkie, "We're at war."

Gizmo looked at him seriously and asked, "Wae who?"

Pinkie shrugged his shoulders and said, "fucking Leeds."

Pinkie smiled at himself, Giz looked at his brother as if he had raped his bird. "We just finished in Leeds. What the fuck did you dae?"

Pinkie who hadnea a single excuse said, "I kinda tanned one of their boys."

Giz snarled "What do you mean you tanned one of the Leeds boys?"

Pinkie coughed, "he started it."

Pinkie smiled and carried on, "Shimmey was chatting up a wee honey."

Giz shook his head, "Then what?"

"Well I was in the bog having a line."

Giz looked at him and said, "Carry on."

"The lassies man walked in and started to have a go."

Giz smiled in disbelief. "How badly did you chib him?"

Pinkie stopped and said, "slashed his face, broke his arm and set about him wae my Kosh."

Giz shot utter daggers into Pinkies eyes, "Great and we've left one of our boys down there." Giz went on, "Look when did this happen?"

Pinkie took his gaze away and said, "Night before last".

Giz looked around Cha was grinning at the two of them. "It's all part of the buzz," Cha said to them. Then lit up his bong. The song in the background was 'Running up on ya' by House of Pain. *'Running up on ya, Running up on ya.'* Cha choked a little chuckle as the bong smoke was being bubbled.

Raymie really had a chuckle 'It could be worse.' He said and Cha blew out the vapour.

"How could it be worse?"

Raymie laughed and said, "It could have been West Ham."

Cha carried on laughing and blowing his bong.

"You're phoning Grandad and telling him the good news. In fact come to think o it that just might be the reason we had to high tail it oot o there."

Pinkie looked at Giz, "How what happened?"

Giz told him about the two boys at Leon's gran's door. Pinkie carried on smoking his Joint and said whilst the dope was enhancing his buzz. "It could be that they were gunning for us."

Giz took the joint out of Pinkies hand and took a few tokes. "It could have been a set up from the start." Said Giz. "That means we got a rat in our house."

Pinkie scowled at the thought. "Ah fuck it," he said. "We've been waiting for a shot at the top."

Giz handed the joint to a young bit of fluff Vicky. Giz smiled as his other hand was handed a miller lager. "Fucking kitchen duty," Giz let out a loud satisfying belch. Then continued, "That means everybody watch each-others back"

Giz finished his beer and went home, growling and snarling at himself. Stating the fact with a muttered "Fucking rat." He got home and opened the door with his key. "Is that you James?"

Giz sighed, "No mam its Gary."

She rushed through to his room. "Where have you been?"

Gary smiled and looked at her. "I told you I was away to a rave in England."

She looked at him with puzzled interest.

"I mean sorry mam."

She began to cry, And Giz hated that. Especially with when it was self-reflection. Giz walked over to her and said "It's alright Mam. We'll always be with you."

She smiled then said, "I know you wuldnea let me down, but your brother James. Has a streak that is as wild as Hell itself."

Giz gave a little nose sigh and went, "I know that, it's me that keeps tabs on him."

Giz's mum was trying not to take it personal. But she couldn't help feeling that this whole scenario was going to turn sour. James crawled home just as the sun began to rise.

"Awright Giz?"

Giz stirred from his slumber. Pinkie sat at the edge of Giz's bed. He produced a bag of cocaine, A good two or three ounces.

"Want a line?" He asked Giz.

Giz huffed and responded, "Don't you ever gie up?"

Pinkies crossed his legs and responded. "what do you mean Gie up?"

Giz snarled and said, "Am your brother right?"

Pinkie chopped himself a line and said trying to sound, straight and sober. "My darling Brother, whatever do you mean?"

Giz's blood boiled and he almost gave Pinkie it both barrels. "Life's no just one big party, I mean you have to come back to reality."

Pinkie went, "Aye."

Giz had had this conversation with Pinkie before. "You need to control your habit, I mean your sat there with the cat got the cream smile. But you got to calm down man. It's a big wide world oot there. And not all of it is bad."

Pinkie lifted his head from another line, "I know brother but I got a reputation to keep."

Giz sighed, "He thinks this is a joke."

Pinkie, "Yes I do," he replied.

Giz sat bolt upright looked at him and hissed, "You even believe that."

Pinkie smiled sniffed and said, "Yes I do".

*

Shimmey got hame at about the same time as James. His maw opened the door.

"Where have you been?" She hissed at him, he smiled and lit up a Regal. His mam just shook her head. "You'll smoke that out here. You listening to me?"

Shimmey chortled and began to sing 'I am the resurrection' by the Stone roses. He finished his fag and went through to his bedroom with pictures of Jim Morrison and Bob Dylan.

Barbara (his mum) said, "And you'll clean up your own vomit and go and get your own Paracetamol."

Shimmey slipped under his duvet and was asleep five minutes later.

*

Grandad woke the next morning with a stunning beautiful lassie whose head was on his chest. Grandad shook her gently and said I got to piss. She raised her head and Gramps exited to the toilet. She lit up as he came back through.

"This is my last day and night here darling. Are we going to hook up again?"

Grandad smiled and slid into his Sonetti jeans. "Aye doll of course, business being the way it is I might get another batch of that Angel hair gear."

She smiled and gave a small laugh. All part of her surprise. She had a way that kept you guessing. A small charm of surprise. Grandad had never met anyone like her. Totally chill. Relaxed and not to define her so easily, she was cracking. That day they spent in the house and then at night they headed around to Sully's house to see if anything was happening. Danny answered the door, but Danny's mam was calling the shots.

"Oh Leon," she started off with. "Nan was telling me that Dawn goes back tomorrow."

Grandad smiled and said, "Aye that she does."

He kissed her gently on top of her head. Danny came through with a couple of small French beers and a couple of Diamond whites. Just as Simone came down the stairs. Danny and Grandad snuck out the back to have a spliff. Danny blazed up and Grandad tanned his wee beer. They decided to gie the blowbacks a miss that night. Nope just plain old toking. Grandad insisted on singing, 'Danny boy, the pipes the pipes are calling'.

Sully smiled as the lull went on. He had a lot of respect for Grandad. And Grandad had a lot of time for Sully. They were pure kin, pure Celtic roots. Sully's dad, an old hard boiled Irishman, whilst Leon's mum came from the old Allen's of Scotland. No they pair of them had rich Celtic roots. This was all good and well but they knew that their ancestry would not pay for their dope and drink. No they had to graft for that. Punting, scamming. Doing small jobs like cleaning cars and tidying gardens. Grandad produced a gram of cocaine and his little mirror, he chopped his coke into two nice lines. Danny went first, he bobbed down and snorted through the little tooter. The rush was smooth and easy to manage. Grandad went next.

"Well me old China," said Danny as Grandad lifted his head feeling the rush. "your new flame, she's away back to Jock land."

Grandad looked at his younger cousin and said, "Aye and I am two steps from joining her."

Danny smiled and blew the hot rocks of his joint, "Aye she's fit as fuck."

Grandad chopped another two lines for them. They had a couple more French lagers. Then went into the house.

"Right ladies," came the statement from Sully. "Let's make tracks, and head round to Paul's." They put on their coats and headed of into the night. They got round to Paul's and the house and garden were in full swing. The smell of Northern lights and cider was everywhere. They walked in and clocked Paul serving up Spatzes to a couple of girls.

Grandad walked straight over, smiled and said. "Hand over the dope fool."

Paul smiled and laughed, "You get smoked with that kind of attitude." Then he turned around and said, "Scottie my man."

Grandad smiled and said, "She's going tomorrow, back to Scotland."

Paul finished his business with the two girls and said, "what happened?"

Grandad looked at him and shrugged, "Couple of boys harassing my Nan on her porch."

Paul stood quiet for a second or two then continued, "And?"

Grandad looked at him and replied, "I sliced and smashed one of their faces in."

Paul motioned for Grandad to move to somewhere quieter, "Well Mate, and this will really cheer you up"

Grandad rolled his eyeballs and said "How?" Paul snorted and said, "They were Leeds mate."

Grandad snorted and cried, "That's all I need a fucking war."

Paul smiled and said, "Don't worry about it mate. I'm top of the trade game because of you."

Grandad smiled and replied, "How's that going to help. I mean those Leeds boys are pretty hard core."

Gregg piped in at that moment, "fearless too."

Grandad looked at Gregg and said, "Let's hope it just blows itself oot."

Gregg inhaled and exhaled, "No after what you're pal did the other night."

Grandad's buzz was turning sour, "How, what happened?"

Gregg carried on "You're pal Pinkie took out a Leeds boy in the toilets in some club."

Grandads buzz was sinking, "Och fur fucks sake."

Gregg smiled and patted Grandad on the neck, "Maybe you should check on your crew."

Grandad snorted and stared off into space. Poland came down the stairs and saw Grandad in a sullen trance. "Aye Aye Scotty," then he motioned to Gregg and said, "Did you tell him the good news?"

Gregg lit up a spliff and said, "Aye I told him."

Gramps's face turned pure Italian and venomous daggers shot from his eyes. The Hi fi was playing Soundgarden, 'Out shined,' *'I'm Feeling California. Looking Minnesota'*. Grandad shook his head and said, "Not Yet."

He then took a swig of his Miller beer and sat and built himself a nice spliff. He toked and spoke most of the night. The house was mobbed. And the music was being generated twice as hard. As any other night, the revelry went on until half five in the morning.

Dawn had a day's travel in front of her and she was a little saddened by the fact that she may never see her sweetheart again. This left her feeling sad and bewildered, she stepped on the train after kissing her lover goodbye. She smiled and said, *'Does anybody Here remember Vera Lynn. Remember How she said that we will meet again, some sunny day.'* He smiled and the pair of them kissed and all Grandad could hear was that song. He walked away singing to himself *'Vera, Vera what has become of you? Does anybody else in here Feel the way I do?.*

Chapter 17

Shimmey woke early that evening. The hangover, well the hangover was a dull thumping headache and a feeling of nausea.

His mum shouted just as the door went, "Kids dinner!"

Then she paid the delivery man for her three sausage and one smoked sausage, and she had ordered herself a King Rib. Shimmey smiled and gave a little chuckle Popeye style. He walked into the sitting room and sat down. Allan the youngest laddie looked at Shimmey and said.

"Leeds huh,"

Shimmey looked at his wee brother and replied, "Aye fucking Leeds."

Allan tucked into his supper and carried on

"They recruited a couple of Chelsea head hunters," Chris The middle brother piped in.

"And how the fuck do you Know?"

Alan sniffed and went, "word gets around, I hear things."

"The only thing you hear is the beating of your meat," Said Chris.

Shimmey took a big bite of his smoke sausage then said, "The pair of yies are wankers, so shut up and eat your suppers."

Lorna asked the question, "What's a head hunter?"

"Just eat your dinner the lot of you" Said Barbara. Lorna gave Chris the one finger salute. Then they all finished their suppers.

Shimmey put on his Crombie coat. Headed out the door and off to see what kinda trouble he could get in. He walked down to Pinkies. Felt around in his pockets to see if he could scrape around enough for a sixteenth of dope. He was lucky, he found two fivers and some change.

Shimmey rounded the street where Pinkie and Giz lived. He smiled and knocked on the door. Pinkie answered.

"Awright Shimmey?" He asked.

Shimmey smiled and responded with a curt, crisp reply. "Aye Pinkie. I'm doing no too bad." He felt a little hungover but knew that a decent piece of dope would see that on its heels.

"Are you holding?"

Pinkie beamed with pride. "Am I holding?" He said to anyone who might know different. "I got ching, I got smack, I got everything you need and don't go to far as it comes down to who you are."

Shimmey nodded his and smiled, "I could use some crack. Take the edge of this fucking hangover" "You'll need tick as well?" Pinkie pulled out a lump of coke. And produced a small ornate set of Pans. He weighed him in three gram. And said as he sealed the bag. "That's thirty a gram."

Shimmey took the small baggie and replied. "Aye, you'll have it by Thursday." He ditched the idea of buying a sixteenth. Pinkie sat down on his doorstep and produced a bubble, a small glass bubble. He began to smoke said pipe. Passed it to Shimmey. Shimmey took in the vanilla smoke and got nice and toasted.

"Where's Giz?" He asked as he passed the bubble back to Pinkie.

"Och, he's doing a small job for biscuit."

Shimmey smiled and lit a fag. The ash would be handy. Shimmey took a drag. "Where are we going the night?" He asked. He then passed the fag to Pinkie, pinkie filled the gauze and put some crack on top of the ash. And then lit up.

"We should really go to Marvins," Shimmey smiled as he took another blast from the wee bubble.

"Why should we go to Marvins?" Pinkie smiled and replied with a small chuckle.

"Coz I aint seen him since we hooked up at his birds house, You know Angela Noble."

Shimmey nodded his head and said with small surprise. "Oh Angie. The lassie who stays in Carrickmore."

Pinkie smiled and went and got his coat. "Aye but you've no tae get any Ideas," Shimmey laughed and responded "How?"

Pinkie turned to face him and said, "She no for you," in his best Al Pacino accent. Shimmey smiled and began to protest, the fact he would never do anything to harm their friendship. And that he was wounded by said slur. They headed to Marvins house.

*

Dawn exited the taxi cab and walked up the garden dragging her wheeled luggage. Her mum stood at the door smiling, her pearly whites out. Dawn caught hold of her mum and hugged her. "Aye my bonnie wee lass, you have yourself a good time."

Dawn smiled and said, "aye Mum."

Mary continued, "was he all the man you dreamed of?"

She smiled and looked at her mum, "aye and then some."

Mary helped her in with her bags then went and put on the kettle. "Aye, You'll haw tae tell me all about him. And his Family?" She smiled and set down the mugs of tea.

Dawn recounted every detail of their first connection. How he had it all and she wasn't going to let any of it slip through her fingers. Not him, not his family not his friends. She was in love with him. She had been ever since she was told the first story about him and his YBC. He wasn't the hardest of the crew but he had shown courage and distinction. Getting into scraps. And powering in with Martial Arts. It was like a Massive attack song the song on Mezzinen 'I drown myself in Martial arts'.

"It's appetized," She had heard rumours how serious he was in the arts. How he had walked the paper at seven years old. Walking the paper was all about balance and subtlety. When he had done it the rest of the playgroup had been jealous. But Leon started a Karate club that year. And had been honoured with the belt of orange, This was told by his Sensei could be stripped back down to Yellow if he got out of line. Dawn had seen Grandad go berserk. She told her mum that story last.

"Leeds boys." She said, "they're no just a wee gang of dafties."

Dawn smiled "Aye I know Mum," then she began to rinse out the two mugs. "If you had seen the damage He had done."

Mary smiled, "Aye some force of nature when a man loses his cool." She carried on.

Dawn smiled and walked out the kitchen and went outside for a fag.

Chapter 18

Grandad slipped into bed, he was in his element, fuelled by drugs and alcohol. He slipped into a sound sleep, his lithe muscles tight and taut. He wasn't fat but he wasn't skinny either and sure as anything he was fit. He had proved to most folk that he had what it takes when it came down to it. He was a serious opponent and that was all you needed to know. Anything else was a bonus, either that or you had just lucked out and been knocked the fuck out.

He woke the next morning to the sound of the radio. It was Radio Two and was the Monday motor hour. He got up and went down stairs.

"Nan," no answer. "Nan," he shouted again no answer. Then he saw her in the back garden, "Nanna."

She looked up from one of the numerous molehills that there were in the garden and said, "Okay Leon, I just wanted here that song by Patsy Cline, Crazy."

Grandad smiled and sparked up two cigarettes handed one to his Nan. "Aye I know who it is, In fact the whole street know who it is."

She smiled and went and turned it down. They then sat down and spoke, first serious conversation they had had. Grandad was homesick and hated the fact that he had to let a beautiful young Lass like Dawn leave. He was two seconds away from running away back to her, He was smitten with the lassie. And wanted to be with her.

His Nan picked up on this, "You know you've done well," she said.

Grandad snorted a half laugh. "Aye Nan I know."

His Nanna carried on smoking her fag, "Well you have got a couple more days before school goes back."

Gramps thought about that. "Aye Nan, I'll chew it over. Try and make sense of the whole situation". He stubbed out his fag and carried on, "Its gonna get a lot worse."

His Nan smiled, "I'm sure you and your crew can handle the heat that they've just stirred up."

Grandad walked back into the house. And turned off the radio. He smiled put on his coat, then went out to Paul's house. Yep definitely homesick, he had been having pangs for home for a little while. And none of this was helping, being at war with one of the toughest firms in Britain. It was going to get ugly. And he had to watch his own back most of the time. Sully was a decent back up man and could call on numbers round about thirty. Which wasn't bad for an under five. Grandad settled on it in his head. Scotland it was going to have to be. He knocked on Pauls door and waited.

"Come in Scotty," he heard after about thirty seconds.

Grandad opened the door and the acrid stench of Grass was all he could smell, it was a nice decent bit of smoke. It had the tracers and colours flashing in his eyes and of course the numb brain was no surprise. Soul kitchen was blasting up the stairs. Grandad walked up the flight of stairs, and the smell was more pungent. Grandad began to grin as he walked through the doorway. Ollie as usual was guarding the Hi fi. Gregg and Breenie were playing cards and Paul was chopping and weighing out a nice bit of rocky. Gregg smiled as 'Crystal ship' came on next.

"Love that tune," he said.

"It's very underrated," Grandad smiled. "Wasn't it the B side to 'light my fire'?"

Gregg carried on shuffling and replied as he dealt the cards, "yes it was mate, yes it was."

Grandad sat down and produced an eighth of slate. He skinned up and made it a belter. A cone, a double loaded cone, he left himself enough for a spatz later.

*

Pinkie and Shimmey got to the door of Marvin's house, Marvin saw them coming and answered before they could ring the bell. "Awright Pinkie? Awright Shimmey?"

Pinkie smiled at him and asked, "Can we come in to your house and rock back some crack?"

Marvin smiled, "Aye nae bother. I take it one of you is holding?"

Pinkie couldn't help but beam with pride. He had half of Colombia, chopped and ready to sell. It was going to be a hell of a night.

"Did Grandad pull of the deal of the century?" asked Marvin

Pinkie smiled, "aye Giz got back the night before last," Pinkie smiled and looked at his wee bubble. "You know we are at war?"

Marvin smiled and replied, "Aye, Leeds". Marvin took them through to his bedroom. Pinkie sat on his leather recliner and began to crack the rock. He had a personal stash of about three Gramm the rest was to be punted.

"Are the girls going to show?" Shimmey started to line up three lines. He took his line, then passed the ornate mirror to Marvin whilst Pinkie lit up his crack bubble and passed it to Shimmey. Shimmey took a pull and thanked the lord for this nights blessings. He wasn't a religious person but sometimes he would count his lucky stars.

Shimmey passed the pipe to Marvin. Who took a good pull and began to feel the impact. He was toasted, he went through the sitting room and called the girls. Told them, "You better bring poppy."

Angela smiled and replied, "You calling me a cheapskate?"

Marvin silently cursed himself. "Of course not doll, It's just that well it's a good bit of rock." Marvin began to salvage himself, "A fucking snowball, in fact."

She smiled and stopped herself from giggling. "Just pulling your pisser, Marvin,"

Marvin sighed and said to himself. "You're lucky your my woman,"

Then an hour later, his doorbell went and there were four tidy bits o lassies. Yvonne, Angela, Wendy and Leah Campbell. They had all managed to procure a couple of bags of Beer and wine. Then just as he was about to shut the door Becksy and Nugget whistled. "Stall Gadji."

Marvin smiled and said to himself, "I knew there was a reason I got up this morning." Marvin let them in.

Chapter 19

Grandad sat down next to Paul. Paul looked at Grandad and saw he was chewing over some serious problems. He smiled, licked his fingers and started to roll a joint. "I know Scotty."

Grandad looked at him and put on his best face, "You want to go back up to Jockland, that honey of a pharmacist sealed it with you."

Grandad snorted, the man was practically clairvoyant. It was spooky. He had this uncanny ability to know things without leaving his house. He was good at it. You would think he would be paranoid. But no it was sorted.

You should go back," he said to Grandad, smiled and said but was cut short. "I'll Direct the money to you,"

Grandad smiled, a strained, confused smile. "It's no just the money. I was hoping to settle down here."

Paul lit the joint and said. "You know you will always be sound down here. Anyway that honey huh?"

Grandad nodded, "I'll sort out Leeds down this end. You just have to make sure that the drugs keep flowing" The music was distinctively toxic and leaving them all with fond remembrances. Pink Floyd Final cut was on the Hi fi. It was a good night and Paul knew he would see Grandad 'Ron Later-ron'.

No the chapter was incomplete. And Grandad's tale had a long way to go. He headed back to his Nan's house deciding definitely. He found the idea of going back warming, or maybe it was the drugs. He also missed his mam. And of course he had hopes of meeting up with Dawn. He went to his junk filled slumber.

He woke and his Nana was downstairs smoking a fag and having a cup of tea. He smiled and reached for the orange juice. Then he got the bowl out for his daily dose of roughage. Special K. He had a small conversation with his Nan that led to him deciding definitely on going back.

"Listen Nan," He said as the conversation carried on.

"What about my protection?" she asked and Grandad smiled and replied, "Danny Boy is just around the corner," She humphed with a small laugh that was dry and cracked like the cigarettes she smoked. Grandad smiled and continued with his breakfast.

"I'll be back though Nan as you know this will be settled up north in Edinburgh"

"Well I never took you for the type."

Grandad washed his bowl sat down and lit up a Regal and said, "You never took me for the type what?"

She smiled and looked him in the eye as things had just started to get exciting. "Your abandoning me to the chaos of the street, I never knew I had a deserter in my family?"

Grandad smiled and she continued, "Your father will have something to say about this,"

Gramps took a swig of his sweet tea and kissed her on the cheek. "I'll be back," he replied then headed along to Danny boys, then, in turn, they both went round to Paul's. Ollie was lying half naked on Pauls front garden. He was smiling and singing 'Shine on you Crazy Diamond' Well it sounded more like a cat being swung around the kitchen whilst his dogs barked and howled in unison. "Now there's a slice of culture you never see, a shit faced Mancunian singing perfectly a rendition of a British classic." Danny laughed and he got louder and louder knowing he had an audience. Then there was an almighty woosh as he was soaked from Paul and Gregg with buckets of water. "Bastards" He shouted as it was nine am in the morning both Sully and Gramps gave him a standing ovation. They stood there and clapped, while Ollie took a bow. "Awright Scotty?" "Awright Danny?" They then headed into the house to smoke some weed.

*

"So?" asked Gregg, "Are you leaving sunny Manchester, Scotty?"

Grandad smiled and replied, "Ach here's no for me. I love the streets in Edinburgh. I mean my mates and that."

Gregg smiled and said, "Good luck to you in Jock land."

Grandad smiled and went, "Cheers mate." Then took a swig of his becks and carried on playing Cards with Breeny.

Switch was the game the fast and loose game. They were playing for 'tokers right's,' who was building the next Joint. Winner being the one who rolls and lights up the doobie. The night sailed into the wee hours. And they finally said there farewells and gripped each other. Sully took each of their hands and shook them.

"I'm off too got to straighten my head. Mum got my orders through. I'm away with the fusiliers Just after school goes back."

Paul smiled and carried on smoking his joint. "Aye that's sorted matey. The money and everything should go through like clockwork."

Grandad scuffed his feet and nodded for Paul to come closer, "Make sure my cousin gets a royal going away party."

Paul smiled and said, "Why don't you join up Scotty?"

Grandad laughed. "No profit in it."

Paul smiled stuck out his hand and said again, "Sorted mate, sorted."

Grandad walked away whistling Guns and Roses. 'Patience'. He knew he would need it. Danny tapered off to his house and Grandad went back to his Nan's.

Meanwhile Shimmey and Pinkie were having a good night. They had managed to wangle sleeping on the suite and at Marvins the girls had stayed as well and they were all over each other kissing, rubbing, passing two bubbles in opposite directions to each other. Meanwhile Marvin was getting his dick sucked by Angie Noble. Becksy and Nugget had Leigh Campbell giving each a hand job. Simultaneously. They were loving it. It was often like that at Marvins and nobody knew where the parents of Marvin and his brothers were, they had vanished years ago. Said orgy lasted until the following week (That being in the middle off said week).

Chapter 20

Grandad left the train at a small station just outside Edinburgh, close to Wester Hailes. Gramps crossed the road and waited for the bus to take him to Clovie. Then he walked down hill to his mam's. He got to the stairwell that led up to his mam's flat. He opened the door and shouted to his mam. She instantly dropped her tea towel and ran right to him Mollycoddling him.

"Och it's my boy back from a long time no see. Did you get up to much in sunny Manchester?" She asked.

Grandad held his hands up and said, "Och Mam stop all the fuss."

She poured him a mug of tea. He smiled and sipped the liquid refreshment. "Och you'll be wanting to charge back into your pals company?" She then sat down and lit a fag. He smiled and she pushed the packet of twenty Kensitas Club towards him. Grandad smiled and took one.

*

Kwami opened the front door and was immediately engulfed with cum, both male and female and the smell of at least one crack bubble, which was still being blazed. He gagged a little as he got closer to the living room. The smell was both sour and sweet, with a small scent of fish, one of the girls was either on her period or she was about to start. He nearly vomited. You'd think that a boy like Kwami was immune to the stuff. Had been there done it. No this was powerful. It was like a brothel and everybody had taken a shit whilst masturbating. He covered his mouth with his bandana and gagged again. It was sickening. Now the smell of Alcohol had jumped in to play. No he was gonna hurl. He stepped over the sinful bodies and went into the kitchen. 'hurgh hurgh burgh' and his lunch was all over the sink.

"Youse lot are smelling evil."

Shimmey lit up the bubble said, "I am evil." Then he carried on smoking crack.

Kwami smiled. "Ya fucking weirdo," he said and took a drink of water. "Oh by the way," He said smiling, "Grandad's home."

Pinkie smiled as he began to smoke the other bubble. "When did he back?"

Kwami sipped some more water, "He arrived yesterday."

Pinkie smiled and exhaled the rock.

"Is he in good spirits?" asked Marvin,.

"Is he stoned, is that what you want to know?" Pinkie smiled, "Yes is he stoned?"

Kwami smiled and responded, "How the fuck should I know, I don't hold his hand." Kwami lit a joint and savoured the smoke as you always felt better after a whitey. And that was the best time to spraf up and toke some weed. He smiled, "it was Liam that told me he was home."

Pinkie sipped a lager and said, "I heard that Angel Hair was good shit."

Kwami blasted himself on the joint "Aye sent straight fae heaven."

Pinkie snorted and said, "Aye too good for us."

Kwami opened one of the windows and the air began to circulate, around and out the window. Yep that was the best move he made.

*

Grandad smiled as he got to the top of the stair where his mucker Toby stayed, He rapped on the door and waited.

"Who is it?" Came the response from the other side of the door.

"It's me Grandad."

Toby opened the door and stood there in his Sonetti T-shirt and Levi Jeans. "How was Manchester?" he asked.

Grandad raised his hand and shook it, as if to say, "Could've been better could've been worse."

Toby flipped round and said, "Jen Left us, and she's pregnant."

Grandad laughed and said, "You'se two need to stop complaining and seal the knot."

Toby went, "Huh."

Grandad smiled again. "Marry the Woman," he said.

Toby smiled and said, "You got any gear?"

Grandad felt around his pockets, he had some coke and some eckies. But smack, which was Toby's usual, he was fresh out of, as the Angel Hair had sold out.

"Well?" he said then smiled.

Grandad pulled out a bag of Fioris about seventy in total. "I can do you a lay-on."

Toby smiled and looked at the bag.

"When do you get your Giro?" asked Grandad.

"End of the week," Replied Toby.

"I'll Gie you ten for sixty." They shook hands on said deal.

"I heard about the Leeds boys," Toby smiled as Gramps counted out the ten eckies. "You need handers?"

Grandad started to chop up an eckie with an old credit card. Then he separated two big lines and the two of them snorted a line each. The rush was instantaneous, and the two them started to buzz.

"Ken what we need," said Toby.

Grandad who was eeing out his nut replied, "What?"

Toby lit a fag and carried on "Cargo."

"Cargo as in booze?" said Grandad.

"Aye," replied Toby. "I think I've got a couple bottles of Lager downstairs."

Grandad walked out as if he was on a mission. He came back about two minutes later. With a crate of French lager in his arms. Toby let him in and went and got the bottle opener. They started to steam into the beers. And Toby said, "You can hae a couple of my sweeties".

Grandad snorted and said, "pit them away, I dinea dae lay ons for everyone."

Toby smiled, "Aye yer one in a million."

Grandad produced a bag of Northern Lights Grass.

"Okay your rollin in it, can you wait around whilst I call Jimmy?"

Grandad smiled, "Is he still seeing Sheila?"

Toby Smiled. "Aye they're going strong."

Grandad smiled, "Are they going steady?"

Grandad started to build a joint, just a plain three skinner. Toby smiled and went to the phone. "How much?" and there was laughter from the two of them. Grandad smiled and lit up the joint.

"You want a word?" said Toby.

Grandad scoffed and exhaled, "Awright Jimmy how's tricks?"

Jimmy replied, "Aye no bad Grandad. You want some sweeties or cola?" They started to spraf, They hadnea heard fae each other in over a year.

*

Nichol left Biscuit's house after leaving him a share from Manchester. A healthy bundle of notes, about five grand. Nichol smiled, nothing like staying loyal. He had a bag or two left he was keeping them for himself. He got round to Pinkies and rapped on the door. It was a nice balmy night and not a sign of rain or wind.

"Awright Nichol," they gripped each-others wrists with immense pleasure. Pinkie smiled and produced a big joint, one which he had made with king size Rizla. He lit the doobie and smiled. "The Manchester connection. Did it go well?"

Nichol took the joint and toked a few times then answered. "Aye you should have seen the talent. Blondes, rock chicks, indie babes I mean uh." Then he hugged himself. "Sweet as fuck."

Pinkie smiled, "Anyway Boy."

Nichol said, "I hear we are at war."

Pinkie took the doobie back and answered, "Aye Fucking Leeds Boys." He sucked in the potent dope, a nice piece of rocky. "Aye I heard one of them tried to chew and spit out Biscuit."

Nichol smiled, "Aye, but you know biscuit, cool, calm and collected, sent him packing."

Pinkie handed the doobie to Nichol.

"Anyway, Grandad's back," said Nichol and he blew out a "Yeah." as the vapour came out his lungs. Answering both the question and stretching his lungs.

"Should we go up tae Grandad's?" Pinkie asked.

Nichol smiled and replied, "Aye, aye why no."

Pinkie put on his leather jacket and they strolled on up to Grandad's. They got to Grandad's door when the heard what sounded like a party going on up the stairs, Lorna answered, "Hello boys how you been?"

They both smiled and Nichol asked. "Where's Leon? Mrs Gratton."

She smiled looked at them "He's up at Toby's. Can you no hear the racket?" They both looked at each other and said in unison "Toby's"

"Thanks Lorna," Came the voice of Pinkie. And they flew up the stairs. They got to Toby's and started to feel the vibes like a hundred people on e's and a's. It wasn't a hundred more like thirty to forty people all buying and drinking their carry outs. They looked into the hall and saw Gramps selling some Grass. He pushed the twenty pound note into his fat pocket. And carried on talking to Jimmy. Who by all accounts needed to know how good the gear was.

Nichol walked right up to Grandad and said, "Your Mucker is here."

Grandad smiled and looked at Pinkie. He then walked over to him and they grabbed each other.

"How you doin' man?" came the voice of Pinkie.

They music flipped on and it was UB40 'Red Red wine'. The ragamuffin began to course through there muddy veins. Grandad smiled And grabbed the last of the beer. Nichol went through the bedroom and found some tin foil. Made a tooter and started to chase the beetle along the foil. Grandad caught up with Sheila who was having a nice piece of toot (Coke) in a small bubble. The party was hooching with talent, all of them stone cold foxes.

Grandad started to tell Sheila about Dawn. She was amused then she handed the bubble to Grandad saying, "That's why you are back?"

Grandad smiled, "Yes she's the one"

"Okay Grandad."

Gramps smiled and took a smoke from the pipe. It was numbingly pleasant. Minty almost. It was this sort of thing the way they made coke into an experience. She smiled and took the crack pipe back "So what you holding?"

Grandad smiled as Pinkie came over to the two of them. "My man Pinkie here, I know he's on that dust," Gramps said in his best Everlast voice. Then as if by magic 'Jump Around' by the House of Pain blasted everybody. Then of course came The Doors, 'L.A. Woman' the album in its entirety.

Nichol was by this winching with a wee stunner called Laura. Pinkie was telling Sheila, Jimmy and Grandad all about his run in with the Leeds boy. Then Grandad told them about the two Leeds boys at his Nan's door.

"Oh they better stay away from the Wester Hailes," said Sheila. "You see a couple of my friends come from the green street elite."

Grandad exhaled at the sheer gravity of the connection. They were undefeated in the whole of Britain. The hardest, West Ham. The party hit Dawn the next day, and carried over to mid-afternoon. Most of the talent had left but Nichol had managed to get the number of Laura. He promised her more kit. Jimmy and Sheila were speaking to Gramps and Pinkie. As the party finished Leon and the rest of them parted company to the sound of Bob Dylan. '*How many roads must a man walk down, before he knows he's a man. The answer my friend is blowing in the wind the answer is blowing in the wind*'.

Chapter 21

Shimmey started work the next morning, Him and Craig Murray had both picked up apprenticeships, one as a bricklayer the other as a Plasterer. Shimmey was buzzing saying if he sticks at it he might get his City and Guilds. They were working for apprentice wages at that time. £35.00 a week for the first two years then full pay when they had settled into the job. They both headed into college in Telford. They were to start with two months in college, there they would study the basic skills of their chosen trade. They settled into their class rooms and began their day of study. They each had a half ounce on their person and break time was soon. Shimmey dived away to the toilet with his rizla papers fags and dope. He started to build himself a nice joint with the soft, black, red seal he had, a potent type of dope that crumbled nicely, he licked his fingers and started to roll the joint. He had enough dope to last him up to a couple of days. He finished rolling and headed back to the back of the students union. Craig was there already. Smoking a nice silky piece of Lebanese. It was a dry rub but it had character. He blew a couple of doughnuts and said, "Want to trade some dope?"

Shimmey smiled and said, "Aye nae bother."

Spook, which was Craigs nickname, smiled and said, "Gram for a gram."

He then produced a small set of pans. Big enough to fit into his inside pocket. He weighed out a gram of his dry Lebanese. Shimmey tore what he thought was five joints worth then laid the weights.

"Perfect." He said and carried on toking.

"Grandads back," said Shimmey he then looked cock eyed at the red glow of the joint.

Spook smiled, "I take it he pulled off the score."

Shimmey smiled and replied. "Aye and now Broomies at war with Leeds."

Spook smiled and said, "It don't matter they probably have enough to deal with down their end. It might blow over."

They then went into the cafeteria and got themselves a decent plate of munchies. Both of them looking like Chinamen. Eyes slanted and neither of them caring if the faculty had phoned the law. The two of them were nice and toasted

*

Grandad got down to Pinkies house and knocked on the door. Gizmo answered and smiled "Awright Grandad?"

Gramps smiled looked over Giz's shoulder and saw that Giz had company. Claire and Hazel, "You are one in a million Giz."

Giz smiled and produced a pack of fags. "You want one?" asked Giz.

Grandad shook his head and said, "Na man just finished one."

Giz sparked up. Grandad smiled, "Watcha holding?"

Giz blew out some smoke, "I got eckies, I got acid and I got some brown."

Grandad pulled out a bag of Fioris and a bag of coke. "What kind of acid is it?"

Giz smiled, "Strawberries double dipped."

"I'll gie you a gram of coke for four double dipped strawberries."

Giz stubbed out his fag and motioned for Grandad to enter. He then ushered Grandad into the bedroom. Gramps looked at the two girls and smiled as they covered themselves up "Awright gals?"

The question was forthright and decisive. "We're fine they said in unison" Then the two of them giggled.

Grandad looked at the two babes. Shook his head as Giz took out the bag with the tabs in it and counted out four. Grandad produced a small rock of cocaine. They shook hands as grandad headed away. He was for home, he walked back the way he came.

*

Nugget and Becksy were having a pint in the Gauntlet. Becksy was talking about the good times they had had, whilst at Forries. Him, Marvin, Grandad, Beefy, Gizmo and Pinkie. He was filling in the details of fights that each of them had had, Beefy was leading the charge by fighting Kellerman a large brick house of a boy who was supposed to be unbeatable. But Beefy had done the miracle and landed him a cracking one two, Then it broke itself up. As the teachers had already been told that the fight was about to happen. Yep some fucker squealed. Anyway the pub session was like gold dust, especially when Nugget was free. He worked as a clerk in the toon at a criminal lawyers, but he loved to fight. He loved to see the enemies of the YBC run and be run.

And the fact that one of the YBC had a hand gun didn't go unnoticed. The police didn't have a clue and by the time they sped into Broomie the crew had disappeared. Up to the flats in Sighthill to one of their many dens.

Saughton were known for their alliance with CSF the casual soccer firm (Hearts). This amused most of the locals and the police as well, most of the Saughton Young team went to St Augustine's, which was a Catholic school. The two schools were right next to each other and were at war with each other. This war had been raging for a good thirty forty years.

*

Dawn was back at work the next day smiling, her bright personality shinning like a new sun had appeared in the sky. And the said sun was hers. She was uplifted, high without the narcotics. She tried to conceal her enthusiasm. But that just landed her in a small giggly mood that was constantly on the go with people cracking jokes and her turning scarlet. She got home and went straight and had a shower. Then sat down and listened to some Depeche Mode (Greatest hits). She was smiling a soft gentle smile and started to sing "Just can't get enough," "Just like a rainbow you set me free". She began to brush her hair and reminisce about the time she had spent down in sunny Manchester. The music sailed through the air. The next morning there was a knock at her door and she answered. It was the postie, he had a large heart shaped box, wrapped in paper. She opened it and smiled it was the biggest box of chocolates from Thorntons. She smiled and read the card 'From Gramps and the YBC'. Dawn smiled and went through to the kitchen where her mam was sat having a coffee. She looked at the chocolates and said, "Can I hae one?"

She smiled and opened the large box of chocolates, "Be my guest." They sat and devoured a good few of the pralines and soft nougat with coco powder sprinkled on top of them. They were delicious.

*

Liam sat in his aunt's house counting his split, he had five grand. That wasn't toffee money. That was enough money to keep Gemma and himself going for at least two months. But war loomed over the heads of all the YBC. And Liam was a dab hand at the violence game. He was ready at any time to fight and fend for himself. He was a great strategist. Played a lot of Chess, mainly with Biscuit. Who really took charge of the board. Biscuit had done a stint of time for handling. The police were always trying to catch Biscuit but he had always been one step ahead of them. It was sheer luck that they had caught him receiving stolen items (a TV and a HiFi.) He had got two years but was out in just over a year. Good behaviour. He spent a lot of time reading and playing chess.

Anyway Liam had become a dab hand at war. And biscuit really liked the guy. He stashed his cash and took some of it to go and score. "A nice gram of coke would see me till tomorrow." He walked out the house in the middle of Calder, and went to the local dealers. He stood at the door whilst the chain and lock got lifted.

"Liam my man," he said whilst brandishing a wicked Bowie knife. Liam went straight for his money. "watcha after Liam?" said the semi psychotic, half naked dealer.

Liam smiled at the dealer and said "Watcha got?"

Sean Quigly was the name of said dealer, he smiled and said, "I got what you need."

"How much for your best Charlie?" Liam smiled and breathed out as he said this.

"Well the dearest I've got is Bolivian gold flake. It weighs in at fifty a gram."

Liam smiled and replied, "I'll take four gram."

Sean walked into the house after telling him to wait there. He came back after a few minutes of weighing and bagging. Sean smiled and handed him the four gram's in baggies. Four in total.

"I hear that Leeds have a beef with you and the rest of the YBC."

Liam smiled and left. He was heading off to meet Gemma where they would rock back the coke and make love. He had no time to talk to Sean. Liam smiled as he neared Gemma's house, A terraced apartment with lots of space. She was on the balcony looking into Princess Street. Liam walked up the stairs to her house. That was ornate with French dressings and ornate décor. A love nest the suited a Queen and all her cohorts. She was a plain lass with curls in her hair and jewellery that was what drove men insane about her. She was beauty and the conservative. She looked radiant one minute next she was noble and cool with a good head for numbers, maths and keeping things happening. Keeping things real. He took her in his arms and began to neck her. She smiled and said, "You holding?"

Liam smiled and fished out two bags of coke for her. The music in the back ground was Love Street. '*She has rose and she has monkeys, lazy diamond studded flunkies*' He smiled as she walked ahead of him listening to the album *Waiting for the Sun*. She often imagined being a rock chick. But she looked at Liam and thought be grateful for what you have, a more streetwise soldier you couldn't get. And she was quite the fighter herself. She was known for her street savie, she was able to predict when trouble was up ahead. Most times she would shy away from violence but sometimes she lost her cool and went right ahead and started trouble. It depended on her mood.

*

Grandad picked up the phone and called Dawn.

"Hi handsome," she said as soon as she got handed the phone. Grandad's heart was banging away in his chest. He was lovesick over the girl. She had done some loving with the rest of the YBC who were close at hand making squishy faces and ribbing him.

"Oh Grandad, oh Grandad, save me Grandad." He growled at the lot of them. Carried on talking to Dawn "You Okay Doll?"

She smiled and wrapped the phone cord around her little finger. She was hungry for him more so as the angel hair was coursing through her veins. It was the nicest bag of smack she had encountered.

"I'll phone you in a couple of days Leon."

He smiled a Sicilian gangster smile, one that said, 'That's my girl'. He walked through into the sitting room and fished out five grand from his socks. Giz walked over and said. "Watcha, watcha, watcha want?" Gramps smiled and looked out five hundred and "Butter me up to the bone little brother."

Giz chuckled and said, "with or without smack?" grandad said.

"With."

Giz dived down the stairs. He was heading straight to Biscuits house with a big old smile on his face, he rapped on the door and waited. The door was answered by Biscuits squeeze, Suzzanne Gaffnei, she was a small lass but everyone fancied her. But nobody had a chance with her, she was Biscuits and Biscuits only. Any fucker got the wrong Idea about her and Biscuit took no prisoners, you would be lying where your shoe laces were at.

"It's Giz," she hollered down the hallway.

"Well let him in," was said and Giz entered.

"How you doing Giz?" she asked.

Giz smiled and shrugged his shoulders and said, "I'm doing no bad doll."

She smiled and asked him, "I take it you here to score?"

Giz looked down at his feet and said, "Aye doll, you know how Grandad feels about getting high on his own supply."

Suzi smiled, "Aye it keeps the money fresh and the competition happy." she said.

The music of the night was Red Hot Chilli Peppers 'Blood Sex Sugar Magic'. He scored a rather large amount of coke, eckies and smack. This was to do the whole lot of them that night. Biscuit smiled as he took the cash and gripped wrists with Giz. They were both smiling their teeth out. It's often in the drug world that when you were doing business and everything was fine you were smiling and on top of the world. Shine on comes to mind. The whole world was yours. Giz headed back to the small flat that Pinkies mum had left Pinkie in charge of. They split the three keys, one went to

Grandad one went to Pinkie and the other was giving to Giz. They kept track that their drug deals were always paid on time. They had locals and occasionally someone scored big. They started the night with some Thin Lizzy on the Hi Fi. *'There's whisky in the jar boy'* The house was full and they were all wasted. Beefy walked in and shouted "Where the fuck is this original gangster. Master of the medicine, cool as fuck patter merchant Grandad?"

Grandad got up from the couch and they gripped wrists. And Grandad said, "I saved a bag of Angel Hair smack just for you."

Beefy smiled as Grandad handed him the small rectangular skin with about point two of a gram. Beefy smiled and said, "I knew you wouldnae cut us oot."

Grandad grinned and said, "That's not all."

He then pulled out a wad of notes and said this is your cut.

"Top Boy. Man." Beefy had been having thoughts about selling Grandad and the rest of the Posse down the swannie. But this act of business had stopped him in his tracks. He felt a kinship with Grandad at this point and Giz handed him a Grolsch. He started to feel the warm thrill of belonging (And if not) running the gang of Casuals. He smiled and counted there was a grand and a half of money.

Grandad smiled as the party sailed on. They were having a ball and Grandad began to feel more lovesick over Dawn. He resigned himself to the fact that he was head over heels with the Girl, but time marches on and he was, well he was horny. He left the party and headed back home. He got into the stairway and looked back along the road he had just walked, It was quiet too quiet. No the tension was still in the air. It was a fact nobody had crossed Biscuits YBC and won. He went up the stairs and opened the door to his house. His mum was sleeping and Grandad didn't want to wake that particular Titan. God knows the sound of her droning on and on about a healthy living plan and working at the job as well of everything.

"Nothing ventured, nothing gained." She would say at the end of her lecture. It wasn't the fact he didn't want to make her proud, no he was keen, but his mind and spirit had higher purposes. They were focused on making a tidy wee sum of money, and splitting the scene. But his sweet mother was sold to the fact that her sons arse shone sunlight.

"If she only knew half of what he did she would put the cuffs on him herself." He said this out loud but not above a whisper. Like I said waking a Titan. He smiled at the simplicity of having such a protector, that was his mother.

*

Dawn smiled and bit her lip, she would see Grandad in a couple of weeks. And then they could catch up, have a passionate roll in the hay. She was just as infatuated with him as he was with her. She wandered and the music was a heart pounding '*Be my, be my be my rock and roll Queen*'. She curved he finger around her labia and clitoris, she was about to use her Bullet, but she was getting satisfied with her fingers and licked them every now and then. She did this until she came. She wasn't sweaty and was having a good orgasm at the thought of Leon's fat long cock. She moaned and began to shudder as she felt around inside her love hole stretching her fingers over her G spot and other spots deeper into her juicy honey smelling vagina. She began to grip her fingers with the walls of her vagina. She had been turned on by the box of chocolates. After she finished stretching her finger she produced a piece of tin foil and poured a bag of Angel Hair onto it and had a nice burn.

Grandad woke to the smell of a Sunday fry up. He pulled on a pair of Levies 501's. Cracked his neck and lit a fag.

"Mum?" He said, "What's on the menu?"

She carried on sizzling the bacon and sausage. "It's Sunday I always cook a traditional breakfast come on through."

Grandad inhaled a light smoke of his fag.

"I'm just coming," he said then walked through to the kitchen. His mam had outdone herself, mushrooms, tomatoes, tattie scone and clootie dumpling. He smashed into the breakfast and was finished in under ten minutes. He mopped up the last egg with a sausage, dipping it into the yolk.

*

Biscuit smiled and him and Suzanne Gaffnie were heading out to a boozer in the centre of town. The bridges where they would meet up with Liam and Gemma. At the Pear Tree pub and beer garden. Liam was smashed on Bolivian and dope. Biscuit smiled at the two of them as they sat there, one with a jug of Sex on the Beach, Liam with a jug of Tennant's. Liam looked as Biscuit came over. They clasped hands and had a hearty hand shake.

"Biscuit," said Liam as they let go of each other.

Biscuit sat down and Suzi went and got the drinks same as Liam and Gemma's. They started to spraf. They had known each other for a long time and the conversation was carried on until they went to another pub on the bridges. But it was indoors only as it was getting a bit cold Liam removed his coat as they walked into the pub, and put it on Gemma's shoulders. Biscuit followed suit and did the same. They walked in and the four of them sat down then Gemma went and got the drinks. Another two frosty jugs of lager, and two jugs of Sex on the Beach cocktails.

"So this Dawn," said Biscuit, "She went all that way just to meet Grandad?"

Liam smiled, "Aye she was a cutie pie."

Biscuit smiled and carried on. "And that's why Grandad came back?"

Liam, "I'd dae the same for Gemma."

Suzi looked at Biscuit and said, "You'd dae the same fur me."

Biscuit gave her a quick kiss and said, "In a heartbeat."

She smiled and they carried on boozing. "So whose gaff are we going to the night?" asked Biscuit as that Sunday night sailed through. Gemma smiled and said, "my pad is closer."

Liam walked out and whistled on a cab. They got into the taxi the four of them and just off the West End they got out of the Taxi and headed off to Gemma's terraced pad. They climbed the stair and she brought out the house keys and opened the large door. They walked in where they had left off, a mirror with a nice pile of Ching. They sat down and Liam went and got some beers, and some WKD. For the ladies. They smiled and said as they took a line, "We got to talk war," Liam was chopping out a good number of double lines.

They were rolling up their own twenties and smashing coke and scraping Magic. Yep it was a good night. "Are we going to face them head on?" said Biscuit.

Liam smiled and 'Rainy Day' was playing by Jimi Hendrix. Liam shifted a bit and replied, "well Grandad and Pinkie have got us two results."

Biscuit sucked up his double lines and sat back. "And they just sorted out a product to sell." He said,

"Is there any of that Angel Hair still on the go?" Gemma said as she gave a little giggle.

Liam laughed, "Doll I told you all in good time. Don't make me get the whip out and tie you to the sink."

He smiled and winked at her as he thought, 'always on the game, more, more, more.' But that was what he loved about her that and her sexual appetite. She giggled again at Liam and snorted her double, one up each nostril.

Biscuit smiled and continued. "You heard about them phoning me trying to noise me up, I dinea take shit like that, you know that."

Liam finished of rolling a joint and said, "it was suppose to have been two cracking fights."

He blazed up the doobie and smiled, "Aye it was two very strong results."

Biscuit looked around the ornate décor and asked, "you still writing poetry?"

Liam smiled and responded with a little bit of sadness, "not so much these days Biscuit."

Biscuit gave a small laugh. "You've no quit."

Liam smiled and said, "no biscuit I havnea quit. You know I only have a couple of passions one of them Gemma the other my prose."

Biscuit looked at Gemma and Suzi, who were gossiping about clothes and stuff.

"You should carry on with your poetry," said Biscuit. Liam blew a couple of smoke rings then handed the joint to Biscuit. He toked on and got nice and toasted. The four of them carried on into the break of dawn. Then Biscuit and Suzi phoned a taxi and went back to Sighthill. Liam slept with Gemma in his arms.

Chapter 22

Grandad woke that Monday at about half past eleven in the morning, he smiled and got dressed. Then decided on who was first on his tick list. He pulled out his stash and counted the money that was down his sock. He knew that a few of his punters were going to complain. But hey them's the breaks and only people privileged were members of the YBC. He smiled at this as most of them were holding their own stash. And Grandad liked it that way. No complications, Just straight profit. And the more you punted the more profit you got. This was the law of the jungle. And right at that time the YBC were top of Edinburgh's underworld, he smiled they had held the top spot for a number of years now. They were only outdone by one team and they were down in London. The Elite, West Ham were the hardest casuals in the whole of Britain. Grandad kicked back in the kitchen and sipped a cup of tea and smoked a fag. Lorna his mother came through after finishing mopping the stairs.

"Morning Son," she said in a bright jovial way.

"You're in good spirits Mam," said Leon

"Aye had a small win at the bingo. And the girls let me keep it all." Grandad smiled and blew some rings. "Aye Mam as long as you enjoy yourself."

Grandad switched on the radio and it was 'Creep' by Radiohead. He began to sing along. Lorna smiled as he done this as he was quite competent at singing and I don't mean just holding a note, no he could stretch his voice and quiver notes. Nobody taught him, he just copied and by trial and error he made his voice crescendo and falsetto. He liked music in general but was captivated by the Doors and Pink Floyd. He loved Bon Jovi and Meatloaf, but was a sucker for the classics. Hendrix, Joplin, The Stones.

"Aye son you're getting better at that."

He smiled and put out his fag. "Thanks Mam but I'll no be on top of the pops anytime soon."

She laughed and returned that statement with her own thought "You never know son stranger things happen every day."

Leon stood and said, "Ta Mum." He then put on his coat and left to go to Pinkies. He got down to Sighthill and walked up to the house that Pinkie and Giz occupied.

"Who is it?" Came Giz's voice from behind the door.

"It's Grandad," Replied Leon.

"Awright Gramps what you up tae?" The question that most people smile at.

"Ach I've no been up tae nothing, just selling dope, speed and Aceed."

Giz stood there in his dungarees and floral indie shirt. "Well its nae rest fur the wicked" Replied Giz. "Ach I sleep nae bother so rest is a mute point,"

Giz motioned him to come in and get a drink. Grandad walked in, "You got any Becks?"

Giz smiled, "No but I think there's a bottle of Miller Cold in the fridge."

He walked through and Grandad went into the sitting room and sat down "Where's Pinkie?" shouted Grandad.

"He's at his birds, how?"

Grandad smiled as he took the cold beer, "I'm just wondering," he continued.

Giz handed the bottle opener to Grandad and carried on "They are pretty serious. Going steady you know the script Grandad."

Grandad gave a little chuckle, "Aye I know the script, head over heels in love, is he holding?" Finished Grandad.

"I'm no sure but he willnea be able to do business. The lass is a bit toffee nosed."

Grandad swigged on his beer and said, "I hope he isnea sacrificing business for pleasure."

Giz smiled and laughed. "I doubt he's hanging up his spurs just yet," he said.

Grandad smiled and spoke like Elvis, "Wise man say, you dig?"

Giz laughed and lit a fag. Grandad carried on with the impersonation "Thank you thank you very much."

*

Shimmey smiled as he finished Monday on the building sites. He headed home. He was pulling extra shifts as a labourer and the extra cash helped him and his family stay in good stead with the council. (And also keep them fed) If Shimmey was anything he was a good grafter. Grandad really admired that about him. Anyway it gave him that wee bit of popcorn money, enough to keep him stoned and happy. Sometimes he would hold for the local lads and sometimes he would keep some back for himself. He was a man of wisdom. And Grandad and himself were inseparable. For quite a while they hung out, Grandad made introductions with the YBC and also gave him an extensive line of credit. Shimmey always paid and always on time. The two of them were local heroes as they had saved one of their pals dad from a house fire. Shimmey looked up the building, and saw the chip pan light up, Craig Murray was there that day and the three of them had to kick in the door and put a wet towel over the pan.

"You never pour water on it, or it will explode," That came as a warning on midnight TV. That and 'Charlie says', the boy and his cat keeping him in check. Grandad and Shimmey were inseparable. Sometime Leon would square some work with his mam's fancy piece. Laying drives and painting and decorating. Shimmey was always on Grandad's side. They were also in the way of the law and they were taking no prisoners. One polis man had a real dislike for Grandad. Kept appearing just after Grandad had done with business for that day. No the guy had only made Grandad out to be notorious. A couple of times him and his partner had stopped and lifted him, in front of all his punters this didn't go down well with the chiefs. This also led to his mum coming down and threatening the law with her lawyer. The polis took it easy on him after that. But this was not over the Polis had a real beef with him. It was just blind luck that the most he had on him was roach material, you know rizla packet with the cardboard ripped. But Grandad had always managed to stay one step ahead of the Law. This was down to factors that I can't go into detail about. But him and Kingo had both managed to flaunt the law and never be caught with their hands in the cookie Jar. But it was steeped in years of mystery between drug dealers and cops with no idea what they are facing. No it's steeped in Chinese wisdom and Oriental ways.

Grandad attended Martial Arts as much as he could. And Kingo knew the streets and knew them well. Christ he looked part Chinese. And had an uncanny ability to be in the right place at the right time. But still they kept lifting Grandad and still they were just short. But this was down to Kingo having a keen sense of paranoia which he trusted. He was truly a master and honed his abilities with a true sense of Psionics, you know he felt the fear and was careful with his emotions, He had Grandad sussed and knew exactly when and where Gramps should be (that and the fact he had a scanner and knew the codes). He would keep tabs on Grandad. Biscuit gave him that duty.

"Look," said Kingo to Grandad, "You know how he likes to keep business clean."

Grandad shrugged his shoulders and said, "I Ken but one of these days that PC is going to get lucky."

Kingo laughed and said, "aye that's always going to be a risk" Grandad smiled.

*

Grandad went home that Monday night and headed straight for his room. He sat down and put on the radio, it was 'Riders on the Storm' by the Doors. He began to skin up whilst chilling with the tune. He finished the spliff and sparked it. He took a good toke of the joint and started to kick back and gouch. He was smiling as the radio changed tunes and kept the spirit of the sixties going with Hendrix, Jefferson Airplane and Blue Oyster Cult.

*

Dawn was walking home from her shift in the Chemist. She had a feeling that everything was going to be alright, but she didn't know what was going to happen. No she was oblivious to the fact that what had happened in Manchester had spurred on a series of events that was going to create hell for her. She got home just as a van rounded the corner of her street and sat and watched as Dawn let herself in. The van had three people from the Leeds crew, Sean Houston, Simon Gregory and Colin Temper. They were going to wait until she headed to her work the next morning.

That night drew into morning and Dawn woke she was in love with Grandad. She left her house that morning and waited at the bus stop. When the red van drove up and opened the door two of the men dove out of the van and grabbed Dawn, they were wearing stockings on their heads.

"Come 'ere you fucking slag," shouted one of them as they grabbed her, she screamed. Then there was a screech as the tyres burned rubber as they headed back to Leeds. They gagged her and they began to take turns on her. They got all the way to a scheme of flats in Leeds. The tears were streaming down her cheeks. She squealed a little as the van sped up. They rounded the corner to the housing scheme just off the centre of Leeds town. There they brought the van to halt, exited the van and went and had themselves a few lagers, bragging about how easy the mission and it was like a mission. After a couple of hours of swallowing down ;ager. They got back into their van and took her to a housing estate on the edge of Leeds. They then carried her into the crack den that she would come to know and hate. They had a room all set up, Video camera and all sorts.

There were three crack heads piping up as she was tossed onto the bed. One of them said, "entertainment" They then laughed, "well lads you pay up and this is free, as we have a score to settle with the lady's boyfriend." Dawn squealed a muffled squeal. And the music started to pound away Dark Jungle techno.

Chapter 23

Grandad was home and having a shower, he dried himself and went to the phone to call Dawn. It rang out, then just as he was about to hang up it was answered by the bleary eyed anxious wreck of a mother.

"Hello," Grandad started to curse himself. "Is that yirself Grandad?"

Grandad cursed himself, "aye Mary doll is Dawn there.?"

Then she changed, "what the fuck dae you ken, huh she's vanished."

Grandad winced as she continued, "you know what, you and the rest of your mob can fucking rot. If I ever see you or any of your pansy faggoty crew I'm going to shoot first ask questions later."

Grandad winced and held the phone away from his ear. She went through the riot act with him finishing with, "and I've told the law everything." Then she hung up.

Grandad breathed a sigh of relief that that was over. Grandad knew what he had to do next and that was tread carefully. But a part of him was excited, the hunt was on, He knew exactly what to do, he was going to find out where the fuckers went and there was only one guy who knew what, where and when. Biscuit, he was a mine full of information.

Grandad headed straight to Biscuits door. Just as he arrived Biscuit opened the door.

"Awright Gramps?" Came the question from Biscuit.

Grandad's face was cold and Icy and shot daggers off the pure Italian type he stopped himself from going pure mental.

"Can you help us oot Biscuit ?" was the question.

It hung in the air for nearly a minute then Biscuit being the seasoned dealer that he was answered, "aye man," before he ushered Grandad into his house. "I'll make a few calls see what I can do."

Grandad went into Biscuits living room. He sat down and produced a small vial of cocaine. He racked the cocaine up a line for each of them.

"Want a toot?" came the question from Grandad.

"Aye man that would be braw," was the reply from Biscuit, Grandad snorted his line then handed the CD cover that everybody seemed to use. *Transformer* by Lou Reed. Biscuit made short work of the line and Immediately started to make a few calls down to London and Manchester. Then after jotting down the where's and when's he started to solve the Police Problem. He was smiling when he came off the phone.

"Well," He said, then carried on, "I've sorted the police problem, well for the time being anyway".

Grandad smiled and lit up a joint that he had been rolling. "But it's gonna cost."

Grandad smiled and said, "It'll be worth it."

Then he handed the joint to Biscuit, "How much is it gonna cost?" he asked.

Biscuit sniffed and said, "Five Grand."

Grandad was in no position to complain but that stung a bit. "Aye okay, Biscuit when do you need the reddies."

Biscuit sized up the Joint that Grandad had handed him.

"Tomorrow, I tell you what," He continued. "I'll float you the five grand."

Grandad smiled and said, "Cheers mate."

Biscuit handed the Joint back to Gramps and continued, "Now about your disappearing Flame. I've got an address, But you'll need to act fast."

Grandad snarled as Biscuit told him the location. Then Gramps decided affirmatively, he was calling all his crew. They were about to embark on a deadly mission, one that they knew could be to no avail. He got right on the phone and called for his crew. Cha was first to react, he rolled out of bed with the sense of immediate action, knowing only that Grandad only called him if there was serious action needed. He in turn contacted his right hand man 'Raymie'. Then Grandad called Shimmey, then Pinkie and Giz. He then got in contact with his cousin Danny. Whom they would meet closer to the Den that was in the heart of Leeds. He then called on Beefy and phoned his Uncle David who would supply the motors including one van to fit the rest of the YBC.

*

They stormed off to the south. As usual they were armed to the teeth and Grandad was sat with a map of Leeds with the house that Dawn was in circled with a red marker. Grandad waited a few hours before dropping an Anarchy acid tab. He was soon spacing out and preparing himself and the three car loads of boys. And a van with nine boys in it. Acheo and Legs and Bats. Then there was Ali Grey, Squeak and Kingo,

Beatie and Becksy. Grandad was travelling down with his main boys, Pinkie, Shimmey, Marvin, Giz, and Beefy. In the other two cars were Lamby and Baxter, Davie Livingston, Kwami. And last but not least Nichol, Pedro and Coleman and his two brothers Lee and Junior. They all had serious looks about them. Cold steely, knowing that this may be suicide. They had no idea what sort of reception they were heading into but they knew one thing and that was it was about to get bloody. They met up with Danny and Co at a small café on the junction leading into Leeds. They were in a small van that had been used in the working trade of Gangers (you know contract workers that did shifts to help speed up the business). The van consisted of Olley, Paul, Gregg, Ian Polland and Breenie. They were armed with two shotguns (Sawn Off) and a load of Bats and pickaxe handles and a couple of Machete's. They got close to their destination and silently ran their engines into the area. They could hear the Jungle Techno playing from the house that held Dawn. Grandad produced his kosh and Stanley knife. And knocked on the door. He heard the music getting turned off.

The door was opened and there stood a lithe looking lad who was holding a small crack bubble. Grandad shoots straight at the lad and grabs him by the neck. Pushing his Stanley on the boys main vein.

"Where is she?" hissed Grandad.

The guy gulped down on the driest saliva ever and answered, "The end of the hall."

Grandad growled the next part, "How many of you are there?"

The young boy gulped again "There's six of us including me."

Grandad took the pressure of the lad and Cha and Raymie grabbed the boy and took him out into the courtyard.

Grandad snarled and shouted, "No one Here gets out alive," and he went in the room swinging, and slashing. Shimmey was next as they tried to escape past Grandad. Shimmey had a baseball bat and was bashing their heads and backs. The five that were left were pretty much running a deadly Gauntlet. At the end of the gauntlet was Danny with a pistol. And a machete. Three of them were pretty beaten to a pulp and dead before they left the small house's hallway, The other two blasted by the two sawn off shotguns. Grandad looked at Dawn who was tied to the bed and gagged and also blindfolded. He cut the bonds on her and lifted her in his big strong arms. She moaned a little as he lifted her.

"You're alright Doll."

She cracked a small smile that obviously hurt.

"You think I would let someone take away my lover, nah doll no me." She smiled some more, which obviously caused her pain. Cha smiled as they left to head back up to Bonnie Scotland. Grandad Held her in his arms all the way back.

"Thank you," She said every now and then.

"No me doll, no me".

They arrived at Inverkeithing and grandad carried her to her door. Mary opened the door and stifled a scream, "Ach my wee Dawn".

Grandad smiled and she walked into her house. "I'm Sorry lad I just panicked, you know overprotective of my young queen."

Grandad smiled, "I'm leaving my two best soldiers with you."

She smiled, "Once things cool down I'll be back."
She smiled as Grandad walked away.

*

"Cha, Raymie you're on Graveyard duty" They then
sped away, Pinkie turned and looked over his shoulder
at Grandad. "You know something Gramps you are
king of cool, charming and dashing,"

Grandad blew a smoke ring and replied, "aye well if
it's personal, and it requires handled diligently. Then
you got me and nothing is more personal than grabbing
your lover."

Shimmey smiled and said, "it was fun though."

Grandad laughed a little and they headed back to
Broomie. They headed to Leon's Uncle's house and
dropped of the vehicles they had used. Then Leon and
Shimmey walked back into Wester Hailes.

Grandad smiled at Shimmey and said. "Things are
gonna change, I can feel it."

Shimmey smiled and asked, "what's gonna happen
when the police Investigate?"

Grandad looked on into the distance and replied,
"Aal in hand me old son, all in hand."

Shimmey smiled and nodded his head and said, "Oh
you are a piece of work Grandad."

Grandad gripped Shimmey round the neck and
responded, "Plans within plans".

Shimmey laughed as they parted company and
went home.

*

Leon woke the next day Invigorated and rested. He was quite pleased with himself and rose to the sound of the kettle and the radio.

"Och son you're up."

Grandad gave a huge yawn and a huge stretch. He sat down and lit a cigarette. His mum smiled and this in turn made waking up all that more worthwhile.

"Did you help that young lass?" Lorna asked.

Grandad carried on smoking, "aye mam of course I did."

He then sipped his warm baby tea.

"Wouldn't you?" He asked.

"You wouldnea be my laddie if you had just let them bastards take her and done nothing."

Grandad smiled, "Toby called in to see what had happened," said Leon's mum.

"Aye I'll go and see him before I visit my uncle," Grandad tucked into a bowl of fruit and fibre.

*

Shimmey was getting his hair tousled by his mam, whilst recounting the whole battle, to his two brothers and little sister Lorna, They began to whoop and hollow as he got good and gory, not leaving out a single detail. Shimmey sat down and Allan handed him a joint while Chris came through from the Kitchen with a bottle of Newcastle Brown Ale. Shimmey was king for a day.

Grandad dived up the stairs and rapped on the door of his Neebs Toby.

"Who is it?"

"It's me Grandad," was the reply.

The lock was turned and chain removed. The odour

of weed and booze hit Grandad first. He smiled "You alright Toby?"

Toby stretched in the doorway, "aye I'm grand, Gramps"

He then gestured for Grandad to enter. The pair of them went through to the living room. And Toby sat down and began to build a joint. Grandad smiled and went and brewed up. A couple of coffees.

"I take it you sorted them out?" came the question from Toby.

Grandad took a sip of his coffee.

"It was a cake walk," replied Grandad. His face turned sinister and cold. Like he had no regrets. Well he didn't regret a second of it.

"Dinnea keep it to yourself. Spill man, spill."

Grandad told the whole story, and told it straight, no embellishment no fiction. Just the blood and guts. Toby smiled and looked and could swear that Grandad turned into the very epitome of the reaper, his face cold and bony. He was telling it with the exact detail of a man that you just didnea cross. The door went just as Grandad finished telling the tale, It was Jimmy, Toby's best friend.

"Awright Grandad, you do what was needing done?"

Grandad nodded, and Toby piped up, "he was just telling me what was done."

"Start again Grandad," said Jimmy.

Grandad sparked up a fag and began again. He finished telling the tale of Grandad's Gruesome, gauntlet and smiled. They then listened to some music and Grandad remembered he was needed down at his Uncle David's. He stood up and smiled and said, "I'll pop round later and pick up my tick money." Toby smiled and let Grandad out.

Chapter 24

Dawn woke that morning home, safe and completely out of reach. Cha was in the hallway playing with his Balisong butterfly knife. It was razor sharp and Cha was and expert at flicking it. He had said weapon since Primary Five. Raymie on the other hand was sat at the front door with a hog leg cradled into his arms.

Dawn shouted on her mam. "Mam"

Mary came running up the stairs and hushed her. "Leon brought you back sweetheart" Mary sighed and asked, "you wanna a cuppa, my sweet pea princess?"

Dawn gave a small, sweet smile, "aye Mam,"

"Where is Leon?" she asked.

Mary smiled, "He had to get rid of the motors, he'll be here soon."

*

Dawn started to panic then stopped as Cha came through, "You alright Dawn?" He asked.

Dawn smiled and returned the greeting. "Aye and you'll be Cha."

Cha smiled and took off his jacket, "aye doll." Then he rested the jacket that was a Pepe jean jacket, on the back of the chair. He sat down. "He mention me did he?" Cha smiled. "Only the famous flying punches that you unleashed on Ali Grey after him punching a boy with Downs Syndrome."

"Aye I was on form and it showed that Leon had heart."

"But Ali took it and took it like a man."

Dawn gave a little giggle, "Him and Ali still pals after all that?" she asked.

Cha grinned and said, "Cannae fault Grandad he's a wee bit of a wise man."

Raymie shouted up the stairs, "she okay?"

Cha just smiled and said, "Ignore my right hand man, he forgets how in deep we are." He then shouts back, "Aye Raymie she's feeling a little better!"

Raymie climbed the stairs and walked to her room with the shotgun resting on his shoulder.

"Awright Doll?" came the question from Raymie, Cha looked at him with puzzled grace.

"Get doon those stairs," Raymie smiled.

"Aye we'll talk later doll," he then about turned and went down the stairs.

Cha smiled, "he's a barrel of laughs, honestly doll."

She looked at Cha and said, "I just cane get over the fact that you rescued me."

Cha's face turned solemn And he stopped her from bursting into tears. "Calm doon doll Grandad wouldnea leave you there. And you back your mates up. Especially when it comes down to sweethearts."

*

Shimmey and Pinkie stood at the edge of Pinkie's garden. The pair of them smiling, there wee pearlies out as Grandad came round the corner. Giz joined them.

"My man," came the voice of James.

Grandad had never been so humbled. He had a true sense of staying. A feeling of being complete. Shimmey handed him a Becks. And Giz gave him a spliff. Grandad smiled and asked, "can I use the phone to phone Dawn?"

Cathie smiled and said, "aye go ahead Leon, but make it quick."

Grandad dialled her number, "Hello," Grandad blew out some smoke of his joint.

"Hi Mary doll it's Leon."

She smiled and responded. "Hi cutie Pie, I'll just take you upstairs."

Grandad blew some more smoke as the phone was handed to Dawn.

"Awright my Honey?" She asked.

Grandad replied, "I'm fine Doll."

Cha sat up and said, "I'll make myself scarce." Then left the room.

They spoke for a good ten minutes, mostly re-assuring words from Grandad. He came off the phone and headed straight to get another Becks. Pinkie smiled as he sat on the doorstep to roll another Joint, As Grandad had roached the one that Giz had giving him. Grandad smiled as the night set sail. He was ready to cut loose. There were crates of Grolsch, crates of Becks. Grandad smiled as he took along pull on his Grolsch. Shimmey as ever was faithful to his country and drank a king size Newcastle Brown Ale. Then as the day drifted away into night. A few of the YBC showed up as the night drove on.

They were all sound, Grandad dived into Pinkies house and put on *Wish You Were Here*, Pink Floyd. Whilst he did this he lined up two lines of coke.

He walked out the house and stood at the front gate as Biscuit, Liam and Nichol all smiled and patted Grandad on the back. Grandad got handed another joint and instantly started to toke. Indian style. Pinkie started to sing along to the music. Grandad laughed and joined in the night was a ripper.

Pinkie smiled and said, "eight nil it sits at Grandad."

Gramps smiled and looked at Pinkie with an evil glint in his eye.

"Aint over till it's over and we just dominated the first half."

Pinkie nodded his head, "aye Grandad, aye." Then he carried on, "If they hudnea got personal, we would be getting it on all sides from half of England."

Grandad smiled as the first side of *Wish You Were Here* finished. He flipped the record and put the needle into the groove. Then got out his baggie of coke and chopped four lines, two for him and two for Pinkie. They tanned the lines and squeaked their teeth. Then went back outside the full street was now in the action. Even the Polis showed willing, by escorting some of the ladies home. They were secretly in heaven, knowing that their presence was welcome as they would have done the same thing if it had been one of their girls. They knew that things were gonna change, Grandad was now a living legend. He had shown by force of his will how to set the mark and enforce it. Leeds were on the blower, to every crew Posse and squad. Every cut throat den just sat back and gave the same reply. "Tough Shit Leeds" But one crew who were on the YBC's doorstep were about to kick on into the YBC's soft underbelly.

It took pleasure on the part of Boz and Mikey. They hated Grandad and his crew They began to scheme and hustle, sell and buy. No, this was a precision thing. Boz was talking to an Al Sergeant on the blower. Smiling and saying things like, "sound Mate, aye mate we'll handle it from our turf." Boz looked over at the rest of his crew. They had done a no bad night of wheeling and dealing. Boz smiled as he drew out a joint from his tobacco tin. He was on cloud nine he had a long way to go including two court appearances. But he had plans within plans. He sat back in his chair and smoked the mellow dope that was black, red seal.

*

The night carried on until the break of dawn. When they all, walked home to their dens. And homes, Grandad went home and so did Shimmey. Pinkie headed into Sighthill to the house that his mam had kept, for Giz and Pinkie. He sat down tossed the keys in the bowl. That was also a coke bowl. But had been empty for some time. He really needed to kick his business into action. He still had his connections in Dundee. He would scrape up some dope money. Then he would pull in a few handers from his crew, Grandad was always up to dae some wheeling and dealing. Giz was as well, he was always up for grafting. He fell into a drunken stoned sleep. A sleep the gods would envy and he would sail on by them in their electric Ladyland.

He smiled in his slumber and woke about three thirty. Feeling rested he went and got himself a red bull. Then phoned Grandad.

Grandad took the receiver off his mum. "Thanks Mam," he said then spoke down the phone. "You alright Pinkie?"

James let the grin he had win and said, "you and me need to talk."

Grandad scowled, then said, "business or pleasure?"

Pinkie smiled, "It's alright Grandad, I've no got a beef wae yie."

Grandad exhaled, "Okay" He said quietly "When do you want to meet?"

Pinkie sniffed, "tonight at eight."

Grandad said, "aye nae bother." Grandad went through to his room and put on some Led Zeppelin the music kept him going. 'Gallows Pole' was playing and grandad was rolling a joint.

*

Shimmey arrived at Grandad's door. Gramps smiled and fixed his hat.

"Awright Shimmey?" The question was neither here nor there. Shimmey smiled and pulled out two fags and handed one to Gramps. He smiled held the fag in his teeth and sparked it up.

"Watcha up tae Grandad?"

Grandad puffed away, "I got some business with Pinkie, then I'm heading through to Dawn's to see that she's alright give the pair of them a break, You know Cha and Raymie."

Shimmey smiled and said, "mind if I tag along?"

Grandad smiled and blew some rings.

"Na man you can come if you want," Grandad finished his fag and smiled thinking 'Everything is roses'.

Shimmey and himself headed down to Pinkies mellow den. They smiled as they approached the door.

Shimmey was grinning ear to ear. He must have swallowed an acid as his eyes were burning bright. It turned out he had swallowed a black micro dot. And it was doing the warm night justice. Grandad looked at Shimmey who was pulling a spook. Looking like Jack Sparrow out of Pirates of the Caribbean. Swaying to music that only he could hear. Pinkie stood at the door and looked at Shimmey. Both he and Grandad spoke at the same time. "Tripping!"

They then entered Pinkies den but Shimmey was more interested in the wallpaper. And stood in the hall watching it crawl. Grandad laughed and walked through to the main room. Then sat down on his leather chair. Pinkie was lining up four lines on his record Nirvana Bleach. He took two and handed two over to Grandad who snorted them. As pinkie put on said record. The night calmed down whilst the three of them got high.

Then the conversation happened, it was a trial for the three of them's friendship. Pinkie outlined a score of cocaine and also a Bank Job. Grandad sat upright whilst he explained just how lax the security was. It was a small town out past Falkirk, Kilsyth it was a TSB and he had the right tools to turn the camera into a loop so it would just play for five minutes then and only then would they go through the security door. That which they would jam a spike in and stop the door from closing. They would then need to keep the coast clear, empty the cash drawers and the safe. Then drive, drive, drive. The score would make them enough money to fund a snowball. A season of coke and smack. Shimmey started to laugh an evil alien laugh. Grandad handed him a fag and that curbed his evil enthusiasm. Shimmey was on a rocket ship of acid. One of the strongest, most potent acid beside a wall.

Grandad smiled and said, "We need to head to Dawn's"

Shimmey smiled as Pinkie said, "can I come?"

Grandad smiled at them and said, "yeah why the fuck not."

Pinkie went and got his car keys and house keys. And they sped off to Dawn's house.

Chapter 25

Cha was finishing of a bag of chips. And Mary was brewing up, they had made the whole bodyguarding job seem as if it was no problem at all, the pair of them were telling tales about the street and about the YBC. Dawn was engrossed in the tales.

Cha smiled as he lit a fag, "aye you see doll, Grandad had to fill his Uncle's shoes and that was no easy task." He then began to tell the tale of some of Doughnuts ambush mission's. "And by the time the Bizzies arrived the crew had scarpered and the damage was done. I mean nobody grassed and they certainly didn't clipe. I mean the whole fight for fun belonged to the late seventies early eighties. They were pure class and knew it to. The respect that they had gotten themselves was pure aces, And Grandad was being relied on to follow his Uncle. Grandad was getting into fights everywhere. He didn't hold undefeated but, game oh aye. He would charge into boys two at a time. And that really got people's attention. He had an assortment of knives, coshes and dog chains. People tried to put him down, but Grandad he was mental and yes that was a state of mind. Like a soldier, like an elite special forces soldier. He was getting bolder and badder."

Anyway as Cha drew to a close on his tale of Grandad, Mary, Dawn's mum, came up the stairs. Cha excused himself.

"We need to talk sweet pea."

Dawn smiled and sat upright. "Okay mum what's up?" She smiled.

Mary clapped her hands and said, "you're no gonna like this but it's for your own good."

Dawn smiled.

"I'm sending you across to your uncle's."

Dawn began to complain, but Mary raised her hand and said, "a tut shh."

*

Dawn silenced and said, "I know, but Mum I want to see this through to the end."

Mary nodded her head. "No doll I wouldnea hae the heart if I lost you."

Then as the conversation drew to a close, the front door went. Grandad smiled as Raymie answered. "Awright Grandad, awright Pinkie, awright Shimmey."

Shimmey gave a tripped out giggle Raymie smiled, "what the fuck has he dropped?"

Grandad Smiled and made a wrist with Cha, "Apparently he dropped a Black Micro dot," said Grandad.

"Lucky fucking cunt," Replied Raymie. "You got any more Shimmey?" continued Raymie.

Shimmey was now at the melting point in the trip.

"Nah man it was the last of a good batch," Grandad smiled and said, "fuck all that, is my girl alright?"

Cha smiled and patted Gramps on the shoulder.

"Go on up she's awake," Grandad walked up the stairs and spoke as he got to her room door "You alright sweetheart?"

She smiled and answered back, "I'm fine darling".

"Did the doc check you for cuts and tears?" Grandad looked over her and thought, 'thank fuck we saved her'

"Och Aye Leon he was gentle and everything, he said there was a slight tear but it didn't need stitching, there was also a little bruising which was gonna cause some discomfort but the test came back negative."

Grandad smiled, "How are my Bodyguards?"

Dawn smiled, "Proper Gentlemen."

Grandad smiled again. "Aye there is no end to what they can dae."

Dawn smiled, "Put some tunes on darling."

Grandad looked at the wee midi Hi Fi a Technics special, "aye no bad for a shop assistant." Grandad smirked and said, "aye well you canae take the loot wae yie."

He looked over her quite impressive collection. "Want me to put some Doors on doll?"

She smiled and let of a few puffs of her cigarette, "aye why no."

He looked over the collection and said, "*LA Woman* do doll?" He asked with a smirk on his face, "aye He can score some blues off o me any day of the week."

She grinned ear tae ear, It was easy to see why Gramps loved her. They stayed a few hours then left.

*

Grandad bedded down in Pinkies Den. This heist was gonna be a treat, if they pulled it off correctly. They should have enough for a large score of coke. It should go like clockwork. It was a three man job. And Shimmey, Pinkie and himself would have the money out in under three minutes. Which was and should be plenty of time.

166

They fixed into the job and would pull it off in four days. They gathered their tools then arranged for their wheels, this was done by Grandad, who had procured a couple of VW golfs. The motor was sound it gave a good growl as it was kicked into gear. Pinkie was the wheel man, Grandad and Shimmey were the bag and cash men.

They would have precisely two minutes twenty seconds. To get in shake down the tills and empty the safe. The camera that watched the door was cracked the night before, and would loop at approximately 9.15 am, This was a two and a half minute loop. And they knew that this would be tight. They were all set for four days Doughnut supplied the wheels, two cars both of them VW Golfs. One black the other silver. They were buzzing all the night before, and boy were they psyched.

They drove into Kilsyth the night before, abandoned one of the VW Golfs on the outskirts, they then drove quietly into the town centre and Pinkie did what he did best. And that was micro circuitry. Electrical engineering. They smiled as they donned their ski masks and did what they needed to do, which was disrupt but not give away anything about themselves. They then drove out to Burger King and had themselves a few Burgers. None of them spoke they just ate their meals and focused on the job at hand. This was the way it was. They had a job to do and settle into the right frame of mind.

"This will take timing you know that don't you?" said Grandad as they sat a little way around the sleepy town of Kilsyth. The bank opened its door as the tellers began to load the tills. The music was playing in their car, it was 'whiskey in the Jar' Metallica. *'There's whiskey in Jar boy'* was screaming out of the car. They spun the wheels and hit the town. Pinkie marked them with a stop watch. They jammed the door then went in strong with Grandad hitting the first teller with the stock of his shotgun. Then he dove over the counter and started to empty the drawers.

A minute left came the voice of Pinkie. Shimmey was finishing off emptying the safe. Ten seconds left they rushed out the door into the car. Then with a huge screech and a growl the engine revved away. And they headed to the other car. Shimmey got out and put half of the loot into the other car. Then gunned it into action. They took of their ski masks and on the radio playing was The beastie boys 'Skills to pay the bills' Grandad smiled in the back of the VW Golf. He looked at the kit bag that his dad had given him, that was half full of tens, twenties and fifties. Shimmey had taken most of the risk. He had to keep everyone at bay whilst emptying out the safe. It was a small, cramped Bank and the customers didn't want to be heroes. So they lay down and didn't move. Especially after the teller took the brunt of the three robbers, her nose bust all over the floor. They had made it fuck yeah. They scarpered and made it all the way back to Broomie. The town didn't even manage to blink. The Police station had just opened its door when the three of them hit. They had no fore warning or anything. They had been caught with their pants down.

*

Toby and Jimmy were telling the tale that Grandad had told them about, Dawn and the Leeds boys. Sheila was sat with her mouth wide open her sister was the same.

"So he left them under his boot," Janice scoffed and snorted a little laugh.

Sheila said, "fucking aye he left them under his boot."

The four of them were close to Grandad, he hung around with them every now and then. But still Grandad never felt a part of their crew. His mother had sent him on an errand and that was how Leon had ended up toking, smoking and Joking with Toby who had introduced him in turn with Sheila and Jimmy. They had been going steady for three or four months now she had split up with her last boyfriend who had left her heartbroken and knocked up. She had the child, a wee boy, Paul. She started to come across to Leon's mums. Leon's mum had taken quite a shine to the pair of them. Grandad was smitten with Sheila. But knew in his heart that nothing would come of it. So he carried on burning the torch for her with no hope. But knew that one day she would turn her head and notice him. But until then he would have to let the embers smoulder.

The tale drew to an end with Toby saying, "I swear to God he looked like the boneman himself, you know the fucking reaper."

Sheila replied, "so he's come up in the world."

Janice took a pull on her bubble and breathed the vanilla smoke out her lungs. "Aye, he's coming up in the world," she said as she hissed. "Sssssss".

The four of them carried on their crack session. They rocked back a good five or six grammes. It was getting later. And later, and they were buzzing on and on. Cool ripping rushes that were a real turn on. Yep you guessed, it they began to spoon each other. And neck and lick, fuck and suck. This was a regular thing with Toby and Janice, Jimmy and Sheila. Toby wasn't that fussy, but Janice was a stone-cold fox. Came right out the film

The Wall. She dressed like a groupie. Fucked like a groupie. And still managed to do the business. With utmost surety and dedication to the business. Sheila on the other hand was civil and calm and gave a damn. She had more to worry her like putting food on the table for her wee boy. Jimmy chipped in where he could but still they struggled.

I mean popcorn money only covered so much, and Jimmy struggled as a labourer on a different site every day. Anyway, things were getting a bit stale, there was no action in the area.

Then Grandad came home from his jaunt. He was bursting with money and drugs he needed to crash. And sleep off the adrenaline buzz. He would have to cook up a bone. He reached into the top of the cupboard. And pulled out a lance and a barrel. He began to cook up a shot. Then pang wizz as the works worked their magic. The tourniquet fell of his arm and Grandad fell into a narcotic sleep.

*

Pinkie and Shimmey, walked each other to Pinkies house, then Shimmey walked the long trail home. Grandad had stayed at his Uncle's for a brief conversation.

"How the fuck did yea pull that one off?"

Grandad smiled and said, "it was all about the timing, Davey."

Doughnut smiled, "you got the dough for the cars?"

Grandad went, "why certainly," then pulled about seven grand in notes rolled up.

"The cars, you like?"

Grandad smiled and replied, "aye they were tip top."

"Good they were my best." Then Doughnut unwrapped the notes, "It's all here right?"

Grandad laughed and said, "aye Uncle it's all there." Grandad reached over and got himself a beer from the mini fridge. Miller time. Gramps smiled and took a pull on the frosty.

*

Sheila woke the next morning and shouted, "Grandad."

Jimmy murmured and carried on sleeping. Sheila looked at him and said "Rocket." Then began to skin up. She smiled sweetly and had this sudden pang of love for Grandad. I suppose it was just a crush but it was one hell of a feeling. And she was in her prime, Grandad a little young (Two years younger) but the feeling wouldn't shift. She was warm and glowing on the inside. But she was going steady with Jimmy. She loved Jimmy, but. There was something wild yet wise about Grandad. Like he had been here before. And she was acquainted with him past and present. She could not stop tying forget me knots in her hair. But grandad would remain aloof. She was a big soap fan, and watched them all. Including *The Bold and the Restless*, *Knots Landing* and of course the king of British soaps *Eastenders*. Then Aussie soaps like *Prisoner, Neighbours and Home and Away*. *Prisoner* was hard to pin down as it was operating on two different time zones. It's all about power in the female max security and certain inmates were trying to control the wing.

*

Grandad woke the next morning thinking about Dawn and Sheila. Grandad pushed about seven grand in ten's and twenties. The fifties went straight into his own account. He handed his mum some dig money, about four hundred pound

"I'll gie yie mare when my ship comes in Mam."

She smiled and said, "cash that'll dae just nicely." She pinched his cheek and rubbed her hand on his head. He smiled and lit up a fag.

"Mam what treats have you got for dinner tonight? Coz the schools are back I thought we might hae a change. Chinese."

Grandad loved his fucking chinkies like. She smiled and Grandad sat and smoked, he was in time for the rock hour on the radio. This was an unusual one Pearl Jam the album *Ten* the songs 'Black, Jeremy, Alive and Rear-view mirror'. He sat getting the vibes of Seattle. It was a constant reminder a small undercurrent that left him feeling good. He was cool and collected. He was going to see Dawn give her break of talking tuff with Cha and Raymie.

He arrived at Dawn's house and smiled as he knocked on the door. Mary answered with a smile.

"I take it she is alright,"

Mary laughed a little, "aye she's fine Leon."

Grandad walked in and headed straight up the stairs. He got to the room door and could hear the crack that was the patter of Cha. Leon opened the door and Cha stopped in mid-sentence. He was telling the tale of Nessies flying lesson when he was hit by a car, practically swung on the lamppost then landed, got right back up walked away as if it was nothing. They were all pissed that night, they had been shotgunning cans of Budweiser. You know piercing a hole at the bottom of the can then putting the whole to your mouth, then pulling the ring pull and sending the beer shooting down your throat. It was a quick fix of beer. No they had tons of tales to tell about the YBC.

Grandad smiled and gave a little knock on the door. "Alright darling?" he asked, then walked in.

Cha was smiling after telling the Nessie tale. Grandad smirked, "aye that was some night. Saughton Pussies."

Grandad sat down on the edge of her bed. "Aye lass we got to talk."

Cha made himself scarce. "You know you've got to do the right thing and disappear to America."

Dawn stifled a small sob, "Aye I know but I was hoping to see this war until the end."

Grandad breathed out and carried on. "Naebody is stopping you from keeping in contact."

She shrugged her shoulders and said, "I know, I just well, I love you Leon, and dinea want tae hear bad news about you."

Grandad kissed her on the cheek and saw that wee bit of sunshine shine on her face.

"You'll no hear nothing bad, and well, America huh," She kept on smiling, Grandad was chuffed and glad she had listened to him. He then fished in his pocket and produced a deck of cards. "These are for you and Cha."

She smiled some more. He then tossed a bundle of twenties at Cha, who caught them then said. "Cheer's Gramps"

Grandad looked at Cha and said, "I got to go down tae Manchester and sort out some-thing." He then said, "fuck the Bozo's" and walked out, both Cha and Dawn laughed as he said this.

Chapter 26

Toby smiled as he struck the match on the box. Then he lit the doobie. And began to puff and toke the joint. He was getting nice and wasted, He just had to wait on Jimmy and Grandad who was due money from him. The Eckies had been nice, not to strong but then not to weak. Just right. He smiled as the joint gave off its Herby smell. Then the door went, and it was Jimmy.

"Grandad been here yet?" Jimmy asked as he took of his coat.

"Nah man he's taken care of the lass, you know Dawn."

Jimmy sniffed and asked, "Any Charlie?"

Toby replied, "Nah man tanned that yesterday."

Toby smiled at this as it was good Charlie.

"It'll haw tae be speed then," he then produced a bag of sulph and started to line up the whizz. The pair of them were having a pretty good buzz when Grandad arrived, He sat down and soon as he was settled he was given his tick money.

"Thanks," said Gramps, "so what are you holding?"

Jimmy smiled through an oriental grin. His eyes narrow and slanted and said, "I got some speed."

Grandad replied, "that means I don't have to charge you for anything we take tonight" Jimmy smiled and handed Grandad the CD case with a couple of lines on it. They then started to toke and smoke weed chase speed and talk work and graft.

"Jenny's coming back," Said Toby.

Grandad lifted his head from the lines and said, "hallelujah, You gonna straighten yourself oot and make a proper go of it?"

Toby gave a chuckle and answered, "you know me Grandad, I dea what I can."

Now Toby had faith, he was always saying you made your own luck. Keep the faith and things will get better. He was a bright guy, he took a home IQ Test came back One hundred and Fifty. This is the same IQ as Jim Morrison. He knew this of course but he never bragged about it. They toked and did wizz and coke all night, Grandad went down the stairs to his house and went to bed.

*

Shimmey was having a nice dream about women, with parcels of cocaine. He was living it up. Speeding and following through with whisky and tequila. His life was just peachy. Since they witnessed the hit and run at the Bus stop, where a woman with a buggy and two little kids had been hit with a car. Grandad ran all the way to his mum's house and told her to phone the Ambulance. She refused thinking it was a joke by her son. Then she realised by how pale and out of breath he was that he had indeed witnessed a murder. It was blind luck that Spook had got the reg plate, Leon was in shock for the next couple of days. He was sixteen and never in his life had he been so rattled. Shimmey and Craig did the necessaries. You know speak to the Police. Give evidence. And Grandad would be head blower. But this was years ago. And it had been party, party, party ever since. Grandad went up north for his seventeenth birthday, and he got a job in a Fish Yard weighing and packing Mackerel. On the day of his birthday they had tossed him into a vat of icy water. He was loving it, he had a good chunk of change that he spent in the pub with his workmates. And occasionally with his Uncle. He also kept up the dope habit. This was remarkable as there wasn't too much dope around. But he managed to find dope. Him and the bosses laddie, Billy scored every payday, It was good times.

Shimmey woke and started to light a fag. He was in the mood for more trouble. And being as he had a few quid from the heist, he was going to get high, high, high. He smiled as he smoked the fag. Then went down the road to Grandad's. Grandad had just woke up, and was stretching in the doorway as he spoke to Shimmey. "Aye you give your mum a bung?"

Shimmey smiled and said, "of course I did."

Grandad blew on the end of the joint he was smoking. "How much?"

Shimmey took the joint from Grandad and said, "just under a grand."

Grandad looked out of his tired eyeballs, "I gave mine four hundred."

Shimmey smiled and sniffed. "They never ask do they?" said Shimmey.

Grandad gave a huge grin, "they need the money," he said. "If they knew where it came from we'd be in clink, dain time. But needs must."

Shimmey laughed, "fuck it, where did you end up last night?"

Grandad had a smile at this and said, "Toby's how?"

Shimmey handed him back the spliff. "Just wondered," he said. "Aye well you ken got tae blow of steam."

Grandad roached the spliff and carried on, "anyway they had tick to pay."

Shimmey decided he had to visit Pinkie. He started to leave, Grandad stood there a moment longer as he began to open the stair door. Then turned and went back into his mum's house.

Chapter 27

Meanwhile In a local B and B just on the outskirts of Carrick Knowe a crew was having breakfast and waiting for the green light to advance on the YBC. There were four of them in total, and two of them were arguing on who would be on point. Neither of them would back down. Sean Houston and Simon Gregory, they were close to blows when Colin Temper told the two of them to "Shut the Fuck Up!"

They were planning on hitting Biscuit. But Biscuit was usually prepared for such an attack. He was a little out of play, you know unprepared, he was sitting down counting his reddies. When the door was thumped, Biscuit thought it was Grandad with his honours (money from the heist). He opened the door, when the four Leeds boys piled in the house and dragged Biscuit into the living room.

"Scottish fucking piece of shit." Came the snarl from Simon Gregory. They then threw him a beating, and afterwards shot him full of smack. Enough to kill a horse. Pinkie arrived at the house and saw the door was open and could hear the groaning of Biscuit.

"Shit," said Pinkie as he looked at the bloody mess they had left Biscuit in. So Pinkie went right to the phone and phoned an ambulance.

"Hang in there Biscuit," he said as he put a pillow under his head, he coughed and crackled out his lungs.

"Fucking English poofs," he cracked out with the pain in his lungs. The ambulance arrived promptly and took Biscuit to A and E. Biscuit was taken right into the hospital and seen as a priority. The beating consisted of most of his ribs being broken and fractures up and down his legs and arms. He was sweating profusely with the overdose, and was going to be in said way for at least a couple of months, if he survived the night. Pinkie sat in the waiting room when Suzzanne Gaffney arrived she was a pile of nerves jabbering on about them coming back and what they would do to her.

Grandad was next to arrive with Shimmey in tow, Pinkie looked at the pair of them and said, "Well that was a nap and how the fuck did they catch Biscuit unaware?"

Shimmey smiled at them and said, "luck." It was a sarcastic smile with the bitter truth.

"Luck!" Grandad piped up, "Someone call Liam, you know him and Biscuit were close." Pinkie stood up and went to the pay phone, he dialled Liam's number and waited. As the phone rang out it was six thirty in the evening.

Liam answered, "hello whose this?"

Pinkie replied, "It's me Pinkie."

Liam sighed and went, "I'm having my tea Pinkie it better be important"

Pinkie sniffed and said, "they done in Biscuit, Liam."

Liam wasn't surprised and if he was he was hiding it well.

"How many?" asked Liam.

Pinkie snarled down the phone, "four and they shot him to Neptune afterwards."

Liam stopped Pinkie from losing his cool.

"How much and was it Biscuit's stash?"

"Three barrels full and yes it was Biscuits stash," Liam growled a little in anger then continued. "I give him fifty, fifty. And that is only 'cause he's used to his own stash."

"I'll be right there," he finished then put the dog back in his cradle. "Auntie, I'm heading out, got business in town, urgent business."

She smiled at the dinner table and shouted back, "aye doll, I'll put it into the Microwave so you can have it when you come back." Liam got straight back on the phone for a Taxi. It arrived ten minutes after he phoned.

He smiled at the taxi driver.

"Where to boss?" Came the question from the driver.

"Hospital A and E," was the reply. Liam arrived and paid the driver and walked into the hospital.

Shimmey walked straight up to Liam, "awright boss?"

Liam looked at him and said, "aye man but I'm no booking any cruises any time soon."

Shimmey laughed at his sarcasm. It was the one constant that they all enjoyed. And Liam was a master at it. Suzzanne started to panic and complain about the situation.

Liam was having none of it, "Listen Doll," he said in an urgent voice, "go back tae Biscuits house and shift the last of his drugs, cause you know the police will be there, sooner rather than later."

She began to complain but Liam was in no mood for a distraught bird, he shouted over her nippy, more than needed whine. "Get going lass, now!"

She jumped a little at the sudden increase in noise. She jumped into a taxi and headed back to Sighthill.

*

Giz was rolling a joint and spraffing to Janice and Sheila, "Aye you see ladies. We are number one in Scotland cause we don't fuck around, we get a job we do it and we do it well." The music they were listening to was Soundgarden's 'Spoon man'. *'Spoon man come together with your plan, come on like it all, Save me.'* He carried on rolling whilst this track played. Jimmy knocked on the door, and Sheila knew instantly who it was.

"Jimmy" she screamed and wrapped her arms around him and they kissed.

Giz tilted his head and smiled. "That'll be Jimmy," he said and Janice let her head drop as if it was embarrassing to know the two of them. Jimmy looked at the wee casual and said "Who are you pal?"

Giz stood up and took his hand into his and replied, "I'm Giz."

Jimmy gave it a good strong shake. "Ah Pinkies wee brother."

Giz smiled and said, "aye the one the only Gizmo."

Jimmy smiled as he sat down, Giz who was obviously feeling generous handed the rolled joint to Jimmy and said, "Toke and a smoke chirppie?"

Jimmy took the spliff and lit it. "Aye good shit. Soft black, red seal," said Jimmy as the joint smoked and left that deep rich smell of opium that you only got with red or gold seal. Sheila sat down in front of Jimmy's legs whilst he passed the joint back to Giz. Giz smoked a bit then handed it to Janice, who in turn took a huge manly draw and handed Sheila the roach.

Sheila complained. "Aww fuck off Jan I hate the burnt lip."

She then threw it in the ashtray and began to put the skins together so as she was first on the next one.

She finished rolling the joint, crumbling the powerful rich dark tarrie into the cigarette. She licked her fingers and rolled it real smooth. Then lit a match and inhaled the ganja. They sat and tanned the better part of an ounce of dope.

'Stoned Immaculate' was the next song to play, you know the Doors. It was from the album *American Prayer*. Giz was nice and mellow and fucking loved the Doors. He carried on spliffing up to the album made a nice wee cone for the girls and a fat baseball bat of a six skinner for him and Jimmy. Giz was in his element and enjoyed the session.

"So?" Came the question from Jimmy, "what happened in Kilsyth?"

Giz looked confused for a second then remembered. "Aww you mean, the bank job."

Jimmy laughed at the lack of memory on Giz's part, "Ach it went off smoothly and timed well." Jimmy relaxed and smoked the six skinner. They had all night to go. The door went a little while into said dope session.

It was one of Doughnut's bairns, Steven. "What dae yie want Steven?"

Steven looked at Sheila and said, "I got some bad news about Biscuit."

Sheila hated standing on ceremony, she lost patience, "what is the message?" she asked.

"He's been beaten half to death and they filled him with his own stash."

Sheila turned her head and shouted on Jimmy, "Jimmy get through here."

Jimmy came out the living room, and straight to the front door, "What's happening Tequila?"

Steven smiled nervously, Sheila spoke, "tell my man that?" so he repeated the statement.

*

Sean Houston and the other three of the posse were sat in a Carrick Knowe Pub, the Busy Bee they were smiling and having a toke, of some nice grass. They thought that that was end of story they had done in the YBC's top boy. But Liam had just come down with a real thirst for blood. He wanted revenge and guess what he was going to get it. He just had to figure out a way to get them to come to him. If they were still around that is then it struck him they would have to be local in the area of Sighthill. 'Carrick Knowe'.

Acheo had just arrived at the Busy Bee and could see why he had been called. He smiled hearing the accents of the four boys. He walked right up to the bar and asked the landlord for the phone. He phoned straight to Liam's and it was just blind luck that Liam had arrived home. Just as the phone rang. He listened to Acheo and responded abruptly. "Get everyone."

Acheo really grinned at this point knowing that not even the polis could stop this from happening. He got right back on the blower, phoned everyone. There was a small army coming together. And they were about to march on the four Leeds boys. There were about thirty of them. Grandad included. Giz, Pinkie, Shimmey, Squeak, Legs and Bats. This was just to mention a few. The rest of them were tooled up and gunning for blood. Especially Liam who was the closest to Biscuit He was thirsty and I mean thirsty.

They got to the outside of the Pub and Grandad began to call them out. "Right you English fuckers!"

The rest of the pub left and I mean left rapidly. Grandad scowled and said, "Youse lot should have stopped them from even breathing Scottish publican air."

Liam was first to go in. They were throwing pint pots and glasses at the YBC as they piled into them with weapons. And bludgeoned and stabbed into them. They had no chance, Liam was covered in blood. The four Leeds boys were done, they could hear the sirens of the Polis getting closer, The YBC pulled a fast one and ran all the way back to their houses, leaving nothing but carnage. Grandad and Pinkie disappeared into Pinkies den in Sighthill, just opposite the Library. They spraffed up some gear and got nice and mellow. While this was going on Shimmey went home. His knuckles were bruised and bloodied. He had done the damage and didn't even get a scrape.

*

Liam got home and started straight for the stash. He lined himself up a couple thick lines of coke. He began to buzz even more. The coke and the adrenaline mixing within his body, he smiled and fell into a deathly trance. He had these occasionally and they looked worse than they were. It was just too much for his brain to handle, so he fell into a seeing coma. His auntie put a cover over him and she went to bed. That night he dreamt of scores and whores. And woke up six hours later, it was half past five in the morning. He went through to the kitchen and made himself a strong cup of coffee. He drank the dark roasted coffee then had a cigarette.

He was fully awake and watching the Scottish news, Yes they were all over it. 'Gangland Battle that ensued last night in the sleepy part of Edinburgh Carrick Knowe. There, locals had watched dumbstruck as the YBC (a local gang) had beaten to death four English tourist's who were apparently visiting family and had come to a sticky end when a drug deal went wrong. The news said patrons of the Public Bar left fearing for their lives. Then the onslaught had begun and at least thirty young boy's from the YBC had beaten to death four young men from Leeds. The onslaught had all the makings of a massacre.

Liam switched of the telly and put on his coat and left to go and see Biscuit. He arrived at the hospital and started to speak to the nurse.

"It's an unusual time to visit," said the night nurse.

"I know but I need to know if he is okay?" The question hung there for a brief second.

"Yes okay Mr Burnette," Liam smiled, as she continued, "but do not make a habit off it" He carried on grinning whilst getting showed to Biscuits bed. He sat down and looked around. The nurse carried on speaking, "he's lucky to be alive and not in a coma, he slipped that last night at about two in the morning, came to."

Liam smiled, "thanks nurse!"

She looked at his knuckles which were bruised and broken. "I take it that was in revenge of you friend?"

"You would do the same Nurse."

She walked away saying, "if my superior see's your knuckle's I'll be hauled over the coals,"

Liam sat down and spoke. "We got them bro' we got them good."

Biscuit woke slightly and cracked a small cough and rasped, "good man Liam."

Liam smiled and said, "You rest Biscuit this aint over." He left an hour later smiling at the fact that Biscuit would pull through.

*

Grandad woke up and got himself a beer. It was a becks and suited him right down to the ground. He started to roll himself a spliff. The doobie was the right mixture of rocky and soft black. He started the day as it was gonna be, a pure delight as the night had been so fine. They understood the people of West Edinburgh that is, they knew that a line had to be toed no they didn't put up with foreigners coming into Sighthill and Broomhouse and doing what pleased. Hadn't they got the picture after kidnapping Dawn. One of Grandad's flames. I mean They should have at least tried to negotiate with the YBC but they had to be hard men. Had to have a go. And in the area where the YBC housed it's soldiers.

There was some rumours about how many troops from Broomie. Some say a hundred other's said it was closer to three hundred. Anyway Grandad use to check himself, make sure his conscience was clean. Not that he was overtly dirty, no he just had a huge appetite for life. This was shown by the way he walked, the way he talked and how Chinkied he got.

He bumped into Kingo and the two of them started to spraf you know the patter and language that you seldom hear out with of West Edinburgh. It was Upside down, it was crazy, it was back to front. And it was known to charm the upper classes when they bothered to visit and score drugs. Kingo smiled showing his row of condemned teeth.

"Good night last night?"

Gramps smiled and said, "it was an honour to do the top boy Proud."

Kingo pulled a fag out and lit it. "He woke."

Grandad looked shocked and said, "they couldnea have tried hard enough."

Kingo handed Leon a fag. "Aye I know, now look at the four of them being scraped of the local landlord's floor."

Gramps lit his fag and said, "you coming a walk wae me, I've got to deliver these Eckies to Becksy?"

Kingo smiled again, "aye why no," he replied. "Good to have some company."

Grandad looked at him and smirked. "Aye how's your brother daine in Saughton?"

Kingo smiled and did the twist on his butt, Grandad flicked his butt away.

"Two more weeks," responded Kingo.

They got to Becksy's door and Grandad gave his knock. Becksy smiled and stretched his half naked body in the doorway. "Awright Gramps, Awright Kingo." Becksy then produced from behind his ear a fat doobie. He lit it and grandad handed him the bag of Eckies. Which were stashed down his Dukes. Becksy handed Kingo the fatty and went and stashed the ecstasy in his house. He came back with the cash for the last drop. It was cocaine he had fifteen pound per gram. The selling price had went up to forty (Depending on who you were) He had twenty eight gram per ounce. He had managed to sell two ounce. So this tallied up to eight hundred and forty.

"It's all there?" asked Grandad and he took the money.

"Aye" said Becksy.

Grandad looked on and said, "I'll count it later"

Grandad walked away and said to himself, "this is gonna be sweet." Half into the kitty and the other half on more product. The kitty was usually split between the top boys and the runners. It could go into the thousands of pounds depending on who were greasing the Bizzies, and how much activity they were involved in. The more they brought out the more the police would take a cut. It was usually, quite a chunk going on the amount of white and powder they had to punt. They did what they could, not to let the police interfere in the business. But pigs were pigs. And one of them was trying sure as fuck to huckle Grandad. One of these days he might succeed, but Kingo had plans and ways around the Bizzies, and that was the genius part. Split the load down the middle, two leave the scene and they take different routes from each other meeting in the middle. Then splitting the run up. Sometimes they would steal old bangers and stash drugs right in the most noticeable of places hide in plain site, old ninja tactics.

*

Dawn on the other hand was having a heated discussion with her mother. "No mam I want to stay here."

Mary was adamant that her daughter was In danger and all the Bodyguards in the world wouldn't save her. She was eventually worn down in the fact that it could get bloody, so crying and just no understanding how involved she had become in this war, and how precious she was to her mother, Dawn backed down. Cha was smiling knowing the lassie couldnea win this argument. Her mother was hard and fast and was not going to back down.

Dawn gave a sigh and said finally, "ok mum I'll go, but soon as the war is over I'm coming back."

Cha smiled at the two of them, he loved happy families shit, it gave him a sense of pride that well he didn't have. I mean that his family were all gone, split the scene. Some deceased some moved on, other's, well others were having a holiday at her Majesties Pleasure. Och he was better off without them. Raymie was a gangster through and through. Brought up in the foster and adoption services, learned to steal, deal and seal the deal with death defying struggles and deadly force. He was known as a top flight button man, there was no one who he wouldn't, shouldn't or couldn't make a move on. He was just the right man for the right hand man of Cha.

They had met at the age of ten the pair of them had started fighting each other and that only happened once. After that they were like brothers. They were loyal to each other and loyal to the YBC. It gave the two of them a happy state of grace. And you know what a safe haven in grace is. Having people who would hide you, people who would stand up for you. No, they were safe in the knowledge that when the Bubble was passed you were always next for the toke. They led a privileged life.

Cha smiled and carried on smoking, "You knew you wurnea gonna win that argument?"

Dawn smirked and replied, "No I know but it gives her a sense of triumph, like she had just earned her winnings."

Dawn relaxed and lit up a fag. Cha smiled and relaxed he was really trying not to burst out laughing.

But the whole notion and emotion got to him. He laughed and so did Dawn. Grandad was on the phone to Dawn's house, just as they were finishing there little giggle.

Dawn took the phone from her mum and said, "Hi doll face?"

Grandad smiled as he knew something had changed. His flame was going to be alright. He knew there were consequences to losing a lover. But he tried not to think about it.

"Are you alright my sweet?" He asked.

She smiled and responded, "aye I'm braw." Then she fell silent like the news was wrong somehow.

"Aye I take it that was you'se lot that were all over the news?"

Grandad gave a snort, "aye petal We were in the thick of it, they had done over our top boy Biscuit."

She tried not to sound shocked, but she was. "How many of them were there?" she asked.

"Four," came the reply.

"I take it there dead?" she asked solemnly.

Grandad breathed out, "yeah they're dead."

"How many of you were there?"

Grandad became sadden at this, "about thirty."

She got a chill right down her spine, "you don't think that was a little over the top?"

Grandad growled. "Fuck no, you fuck with the bull and you get the horns."

She laughed a little at this statement, "when will this war end?"

Grandad stopped himself from cursing and said, "hopefully this will settle everything. I mean you dinea just waltz into someone's home ground, put their top boy on the critical conditions list, sit back and laugh as though you had won the war."

Dawn gave a little squeak and said, "no I don't suppose you dae."

They chatted for another ten, fifteen minutes at which they discussed Dawn's departure to the USA. Grandad was really sweet about the whole thing promising to stay in touch. Grandad said goodbye but before he did he spoke with Cha.

"Aye Grandad, aye," as Grandad told him the good news about Biscuit. "Hard as nails," was the response to the statement. They said their goodbyes then hung up.

Cha turned round and said, "Me and Raymie have to wait and see you off before we can go back to Broom toon."

Dawn smiled, "Aye well I'd like to have a day alone with Grandad before I bid you bon voyage."

Mary was listening at the top of the stairs, "aye okay Lass, I suppose I owe you that at least," she said as she walked into her daughters room.

Cha smiled, "that's love for you," he said. thing was the perfect gentleman. Raymie on the other hand was always out of his tree, constantly on the hustle and constantly watching Cha's back. If one of them got pinched then the other would hand himself in at the same time. They started off getting acquitted from the Sherriff, then they just abused the system made it an escape. That's why they call it the cooler, they knew one thing that someday they would be classed ba all the other inmates were classed, institutionalised was what the Doctor called it. I mean they were hard core gangsters, but they didn't need reminding, no they had it tattooed into them. The pair of them had matching tatt's on their hands ACAB. This stood for All Cops Are Bastards. They were well known in the judicial system. They just couldn't keep on the straight and narrow. And that's why YBC revered them.

*

The night was cooling down until it rained gently, Grandad was looking out his window at the gentle rain. He smiled and took a draw of his joint feeling the rain patter on the window pain. It was a decent night, not too hot and not too cold. Just a cool breeze.

Sheila appeared under his window. "You just keep getting smoother by the day," she shouted.

Grandad broke into a wide grin. "Ach lass, it's what needs done."

She blew Grandad a kiss and disappeared into the night. Grandad smiled some more and fished out his lance and barrel. He was getting to be the right little pin head. He was also running out of kit. But this would be rectified by tomorrow, He would pay wee Nichol a visit. Craig was one of those lads you knew were straight wae yie, if he didn't like you he would say something like "Fuck you your face don't fit" If you didn't take that hint you were liable for stitches. And Nichol never let the same guy try that twice, if your bottle didn't crash and that was crucial and you had already had a warning from Nichol, you were as good as dead. I mean the scrappies were right on the intersection between Forrester and Broomhouse, You just dinea mess wie the YBC. They sealed your fate. Then gone, 'Tombs of Rust' you had to have a hard spirit coming from Broomhouse and that was sprayed all over the flats,

Vandals were the least of your worries if you didn't fit in or if the thieves got sight of you well …

Polis you say, they hate even going into that area, and gangs run all day and all night, some times they rumbled, other times they kept there heeds doon. Grandad was listening to the Doors as he fell asleep, 'Riders on the Storm'. Being the favourite of his. It just chilled Grandad out. That song in particular. He slept whilst the CD played, it was the *Best of the Doors* came out the same time as the movie with Val Kilmer. Grandad was instantly hooked on the Doors. After seeing the performance By Meg Ryan and Val Kilmer. Grandad slept on.

Chapter 28

The next morning arrived and Grandad was feeling invigorated. That fix at night helped him sleep it was a miracle cure, No pain, no ache in his bones. Just the warm smaky rush that lasted the whole night, no babies didn't sleep as well as Grandad after he shot up. The daylight was here and Grandad was in full conscience, He stashed his works then got on with his day. He would have to go into town and visit Biscuit. He dressed then hit the road. Going straight into the hospital and straight up to the reception

"I'm here to visit Ally Tilley." he asked. the nurse smiled and asked, "friend or family?"

Grandad relaxed, "friend," he replied.

The nurse took a look at her manifest and said, "Ward four."

Grandad wandered in the direction of Biscuits bed. Grandad got there and sat down in the seat next to his bed.

"Biscuit psst Biscuit, you see the hoochie round here?"

Biscuit woke slightly, "aye Grandad I see the hoochie round here."

Grandad gave a chuckle and said, "I wonder how much it is, I mean I could murder a blow job?"

Biscuit stirred a little, "Grandad keep your pecker in your pants."

"Grandad you got a girl."

Gramps smiled and carried on, "och she's banged up and you know needs must."

Biscuit broke a half smile half laugh. "Anyway did you bring grapes?" Asked Biscuit.

"No man, But I brought you a pack o fags and a wee bit dope."

Biscuit laughed again, "How the hell I'm I gonna skin up here?"

The question didn't surprise Grandad, but the solution to the question that was the only way Biscuit was getting a smoke. "You'll need to dive into the toilet, skin up then bring it to me"

Grandad hadnea really thought it through but he was right it was the only solution. So he did so.

*

Grandad headed home after completing said task. He got round to his house and the police were there waiting for him. First thing he did was stash his narcotics. Then he walked up to the stairwell. The constable got out his car and walked straight towards him. Grandad snarled on one side of his face. The officer in charge was coming down the stairwell with Shimmey in handcuffs.

He too was snarling. "The pair of you Robbery."

Grandad humphed. "Honest sir I don't know what you are talking about," said Gramps to the statement.

Shimmey smiled and giggled, "Someone grass us boss?"

The officer looked at him and said, "I canea divulge that information." They were then put into the meat wagon and away to St Leonards police station in the heart of the city. There they would stay until the end of the weekend. This was a major hassle for the two of them as they knew Pinkie might just slip through the net and avoid being huckled. If he did then the score was still in they're favour. They just had to stay silent not a peep out of either of them. This would be a cake walk. They had two days to keep stum. The PF had a real hardon for them. It wasn't just they two but the whole of the YBC. He was expected to get results especially after the massacre in Carrick Knowe. He had a list of thirty or so serious offenders and twelve or so juveniles. It was going to be a major shake down, with no one being left alone. And all the I's and dots being made of high importance. No fact would be left out no evidence would be left out. It was gonna be a real stinker of a weekend.

*

Pinkie heard the scanner finalise the operation, they were all green to go. Pinkie did what any sane person would do and get the fuck out of Dodge. He headed to Dundee. To his connection. Whom he had built up a nice little business with. Willie Briggs. Willie wasn't your average dealer no, he was a trained martial artist had a serious collection of knives. Some rare Indonesian blades, a Khukri with a dragon etched on the blade. Anyway he put in the call asking if he could hole up in a safe house in Dundee.

"Aye Briggie just until this all blows over." He said and wondered who had grassed them all in.

Briggie smiled at the position he was in and replied, "aye Pinkie. You've been nothing but good luck tae us."

Pinky breathed out in relief. Willie was the man of the hour, he was a good contact and had lots of connections, he was also totally chill cool as it comes. He had done time but didn't wallow in it even when things were going well. He was sound, reliable and highly thought of. Pinkie took down the address of the safe house in Dundee.

"I'll meet you there said Briggie."

Pinkie thanked his lucky stars, and headed off to get the train through to Dundee. He was sharpish as about five minutes after he left the Bizzies were at his mum's door. She told them nothing, and they were about to lean on her slightly but Giz walked in.

"Whats the polis daen here mam?" He gulped suddenly as he knew they were here for his brother. But knowing the script they would be satisfied with him. He smiled as they read him his rights. It's not like he hadn't heard them before. They took him also to St Leonards, he started smiling when he heard Grandads voice.

"Grandad," Said Giz.

Gramps replied, "Giz my main man."

Shimmey started to laugh, "Only one more to come," Giz laughed back,

"They'll no get my brother that easily," said Giz.

Grandad spat a groger down the steel pan. "Aye I know but that dusnea answer the question, Who's the rat?"

Giz breathed out, "It dusnea matter for the time being, it looks like we are all going doon."

Grandad asked the question that they all needed to know, "where do you think they will send us?"

Giz laughed at this "The only place they send teenage laddies."

Grandad smiled, "Polmont."

"But first we have to put in an appearance," Giz laughed.

"I hope McCrann gets us a deal."

"Any way what you looking at Gramps?" Grandad smiled and responded, "About four to five years If they've got me pinned down. But McCrann is a good brief he got people of with more on their plates." Grandad sighed. "Anyway we are well out of it, they got nothing"

Shimmey laughed, "aye I ken," he said.

"We could end up on remand," Grandad laughed. "They usually knock that time of your sentence." The polis man came by and tossed them all a Fish supper.

"Cheers boss." They all said as they tucked into they're scran. They had a long uncomfortable two days to wait. Then they would either be incarcerated or they would walk. Any how it didn't matter, as well as the three of them were like a mini strike force. They could scrap, adapt and blast their way out. And I mean that in the biblical sense. I mean epic.

*

Pinkie arrived at the flat he was told to go too, He arrived and Brigg answered the door and handed him a beer and a spliff. "Come in buddy? Come in.?" He walked into the flat and was instantly recognised. He had a sports bag full of clothes, and a stash of dope and down his sock he had seven grand. He handed Briggy three grand for the courtesy, but that came out his pocket and not his stash money. He sat down and Briggy spoke to the Gadji whose house he was in.

"He Liam's Pal?"

Briggy smiled, "aye and nae hassle."

Then he handed the guy, half of the three grand. The guy walked over to Pinkie smiled and said, "My names Colin but you can call me Cole."

Pinkie smiled a sharp slick smile, one you had to be quick to catch. "Pinkie," came the reply From James.

"Aye man," said Cole, "I hear you just pulled a score."

Pinkie laughed, "aye and went to war," he said.

Cole liked him more and more. "If you got any drugs sharing's caring," said Cole.

Pinkie looked on at the table that had more drugs than the local Chemists. Pinkie breathed a sigh of relief and got wired in there. Briggy sat part of the night listening to Pinkie recount the war with Leeds. And the heist. He usually didn't go out on a limb like that but what the hell he had nothing else to do. The ladies were away in their dreamy way. Like Elvis Presley he had an auror a captivating way. But the night sailed through until morning. Pinkie went through to the bedroom that he had been allocated by Cole, He lay down and fell into a narcotic sleep. With vodka as a pillow. He slept as the house settled down. This was a first class dealership. They had lots of money and lots of drugs. You'd think a place like that would be busted, nope they didn't even catch them with their pants down. No they had informants in the police. But Pinkie made himself at home.

In Coles house, he wanted for nothing, food, alcohol and of course drugs. He figured that if they didn't catch him first, he would go down to Manchester. In a couple of days or so. He phoned Paul Kelley the following evening. Paul answered practically straight away.

"Awright, Paul here," Pinkie had only heard of Paul, he was like a Guru to Grandad. And Grandad spoke highly of him and the rest of the Quality Street gang, He liked it down there. Pinkie never thought much about it. Pinkie responded to Paul.

"Hi is that Paul?"

Paul smiled that wicked joker smile. "Yes mate you one of Grandads crew?"

Pinkie smiled back, "yes it's me Pinkie."

Paul Carried on grinning, "nice one mate," he said to someone who had handed him a joint.

"Ah yes Pinkie, Grandad's right hand man am I right?"

Pinkie shook his head, "listen mate we need to meet."

Paul sucked in some of the joint he had in his hand, "what's it about?"

Pinkie spilled. "We are in a mess, the Bizzies have busted everyone that had anything to do with the Leeds massacre."

Paul carried on toking his joint, "well that's good to know coz I was at the raid for Dawn." Pinkie laughed, "So was I"

"I tell you what seeing as though you are on the run, I'll help any way I can."

Pinkie shook his head in agreement, "I'll be down in a few days."

Paul smiled and they both hung up. Paul walked away whilst the Temptations 'Pappa was a Rolling Stone' came on the Hi Fi.

Danny screamed out "Tune!" and the night carried on with a heavy smoke session. Pinkie carried on with his drug fuelled' run, he would probably be doing this till next month. You would think that he would calm down.

But the only way was the old way, tie yourself to the mast my friend and the storm will end. That song lyric was bang on especially whilst your buddies were looking at a healthy sentence. Pinkie knocked back some tequila, and snorted two lines of coke. He was just about to lite up a fag when the Verve came on the Hi Fi. He sat and listened the songs were full of emotion and held you captive, right time, right moment, right place.

*

Grandad, Shimmey and Giz were put in the holding cells under the Sheriff court in the centre of Edinburgh. Shimmey was first to be tried. He stood there on the dock waiting for the Sheriff to raise his head.

"Okay Mr John Feggans, It seems as if it was only last week you were up in front of me am I correct?"

Shimmey was in fact a month away from finishing his good behaviour bond.

"Well young man that will go against you."

Shimmey couldn't bear to have been seen as a suck up anyway, he smiled inside.

"You, I am giving full custodial sentence of five months." Shimmey looked up and said before he was taken away "YBC."

The whole court laughed except the Sheriff who said, "make that seven months, Polmont, take him away".

Grandad was next, He walked up the stairs to the courtroom "Ah Mr Pitter Patter Gratton Still a thieve I see."

Grandad laughed as that was the name his guidance teacher had called him. "Yes your honour. I mean well I'm trying your honour."

The Sherriff gave a grave hrumph. The Brief for Grandad and the other two tried an emotional plea on all the defendants but the Sherriff was immune to the man's plea's.

"A year two months for you, seeing as it's obvious you are the brains of your little outfit."

Grandad snarled but lucky for him the Sherriff was busy reading the next docket. He was taken back down to the cells where they would make the journey to Polmont young offenders institution. But Giz was next to come up. Young Gary Williamson smiled a row of sharks teeth beaming as though he had just stumbled on the virgin Marys underwear and the Sherriff was wearing said knickers. He beamed fully at the whole courtroom "You are just a snack boy, two months."

He dismissed the court room and Giz was taking down to the cells And they were cuffed and booted for the trip to Polmont.

*

Kingo who had witnessed the capture of both Shimmey and Grandad. He put in the call to McCrann's office, his secretary answered. "McCrann's office how may I help you?"

Kingo relaxed and asked, "what did the two of them get custodial or what?"

She smiled and answered, "You mean the three of them as Giz was arrested the same night."

Kingo laughed and asked, "What was the end result doll?"

"Well Grandad took the brunt of the sentencing He got a year two months, Giz got the least two months,

And Shimmey he got seven months it was five but Shimmey chanted the YBC and he wasn't amused."

Kingo laughed at the fact that Shimmey had never done anything to make his life easy, especially when it came to the law.

"Did they mention a witness or informant?"

The secretary smiled at this. "There was a document with a witness's testimony. But they were not able to say the name of said witness as they were already in protective custody."

Kingo looked restless at this, "will they ever uncover this witness or is it just a one-time venture?" He asked.

The secretary responded, "that document will remain sealed and confidential."

Kingo laughed at the statement. "That figures," he said after thinking on that this rat that's cutting about and they can't stop them. They even had a hand in Kingo's brothers jail sentence.

"Is this the same grass who had my brother over a barrel?" asked Kingo.

She smiled and said, "Leave it with me, then call back in two days."

"Thanks Doll," said Kingo then he hung up. Now he was getting somewhere. Pinkie was also getting somewhere. He had rung around the top boys of the YBC, seeing who was in the clink and who wasn't. A fair amount of the YBC had been huckled and they didn't stand a chance with the various diets and warrants. No at least twenty had been pulled, and the rest were looking at a similar fate. No hard times will come especially when they were at war. And Leeds weren't done with yet. No they were planning a raid on the so called Quality Street Gang. But Paul was ready for them, he was gathering his troops and was setting a little trap of his own. He was ready for them, he just had to set the bait. Danny boy was who he was thinking, he was the obvious choice, being as he was Scotty's cousin and the right choice as they would obviously focus on him.

The vans were circling Danny's house, he was aware of this but didn't let it sour his high with paranoia. No he smiled all the way he was certain his back was covered. But this didn't matter as after the school was finished he was joining the army. This was giving him an immediate effect. If he timed it right he could be, away in the army and Scott free. Danny was about to make his move. He had been aware of the Vans for about a week now. Most people would have dismissed it as coincidence. But Danny, who was as sly as they appeared, didn't make a meal of it he led the van like a lamb to slaughter. Round the back of Parrenthorn. Down to a small piece of ground that was derelict and ideal for his purposes. He had made the plan without leaving a single thing to chance. Even Reini Gigiceo was wanting in. Paul and Gregg were hiding at the side of the tunnel that led to a barren piece of ground where the rest of them hid between a large concrete block and a mound of grass.

They were tooled up to the eyeballs. Swords, machete's and a good old fashioned shooter, Paul was the one with the double barrel shotgun. They all stood their ground waited as Sully drew the van into his clutches. Then turned and smiled at them as seven boys vacated the van. They walked carefully as Sully backed up to the boulder and the Leeds crew advanced.

"Where's your fucking cousin, the scummy Jock. Grandad is his name."

Sully's face turned stonelike and grim. Then with a fierce whistle. The ten boys that lay in waiting were suddenly active in the battle. One of the Leeds boys took it both barrels from Paul. Breenie was attached to one of their faces and was biting his fucking nose off. Blood everywhere. Sully kicked one of them in the bollocks with his Timbies. Then smashed his face in with rapid speed punches.

Olly was fighting two at once, no fear. He was swinging his Japanese Katana at two of them. They were lucky to begin with but Olly was faster than them and one fell and three fingers went flying by and the boy that was keeping Olly at bay turned green as Olly sliced his partner across the throat with the Katana. The rest of them got the treatment. Paul was on the side lines having a smoke "This is better than sex" said Paul as he struck a match. There was blood everywhere. Slick red and pieces, pieces everywhere. Sully sat next to Paul and took a toke of his joint.

"Well problem solved," came the chuckling voice of Sully, They tossed a coin at the one who took the least of punishment, And Paul said, "You'll need that, to contact your next of kin." Sully walked home knowing that that was it over. They were just only so many tanking's they could take. They had been out classed, and out smarted.

*

Pinkie carried on drinking and talking about the hustles he had done and the fights he had won. He hadn't heard from Kingo or any of the rest of the YBC. And he was sure Grandad and Shimmey were in the YO's Polmont.

Two hours later the phone rang. It was getting dark and summer was almost gone and Kingo had picked up the number from Paul Kelley. Whilst he had been on the phone to him. Paul had told him about the little ruck they had with Leeds. And he smiled as Paul finished and told him Pinkies number.

"Dae yea think that this rat is working both sides of the border?" Asked Kingo.

Paul's smile faded, "I'm close to getting this cheese eating freak."

Kingo Cheered up. He now knew that it wasn't only him on the trail. He said bon voyage then phoned Pinkie, Pinkie took the call through the room.

"What do you mean Giz has went down as-well?"

"How the fuck did they get hold of Giz?"

"I thought you were keeping an eye on the law?" Pinkie carried on, "I mean for fuck sakes He is one of our best fighters."

Kingo winked at his bird, "Aye I know but this rat is working both sides of the border." Kingo smiled and said, "My brother is out in a few days, He's got a nose for fuckers like that."

Pinkie Smiled, "thank fuck someone is making progress!" said Pinkie. "You better phone his flame and tell her the bad news".

"Why don't you phone her?" said Kingo.

Pinkie snarled, "just phone her Kingo. I mean they have probably got her Phone tapped. And Kingo use a public phone;"

"Good thinking Pinkie."

"Oh fur fuck sakes!" Said Cha. "Who the fuck dae yea think you're talking tae Kingo?"

Kingo gulped. "Right Kingo take it fae the top?"

Kingo breathed a little easier. "Grandad took the brunt of the convictions, fourteen months, And Shimmey got seven after mouthing off. Giz was just a snack he got two months."

"Are you gonna tell her, Aye or no?" Kingo felt the back of his neck stand straight.

"You'd be better to tell her." said Kingo. "Aye I know you dinea want any messed-up bird greeting on at you?"

Cha hung up the phone. Raymie came up the stair with a couple of mugs of tea. Raymie asked the question, "How much longer are we gonna be here?"

Cha who was a little vacant at the time shook himself then responded, "That's Grandad and Shimmey, huckled along wae Gizmo."

Raymie took a sip of his tea "I take it that means Dawn will no get to say goodbye?" said Raymie.

Cha smiled, "Any way we only got a couple of more days then Dawn will be on her way to America".

*

Grandad was immediately surrounded by the sheer cold fact. He was in prison, him and his two friends, they were just in, but someone must have told the rest of the place that they were coming. "Fuck you and your YBC" was shouted as they headed to their cells. They were outnumbered but Grandad was sure he didn't have a beef with anyone and they were just winding him. Shimmey and Giz up.

Grandad settled in his grey cell. As did Giz and Shimmey. They were going to do hard time. And sure as fuck, Leeds will have put a price on their heads. They future in that toilet was very bleak. Very bleak indeed, they would have every gang in Scotland, trying to make a name for itself. Not to mention the fights that certain casuals were left bleeding by the YBC, no this wasn't a cake walk. They had a lot to contend with, but you know what Grandad liked those odds. He had a firm grip on himself to know that he was to expect the unexpected. They were outnumbered at least three to one. He could hear in the distance Cyprus Hill 'Aint going out like that, aint going out like that' He had to procure himself a radio preferably one with a CD player. He knew that if he behaved and didn't start any trouble he would be out in just over half the time. Shimmey would to, and Gizmo well like what the Sheriff said he was just a snack. Giz just shrugged as the three of them were locked down. Grandad smiled and started to sing along to the Cyprus hill album "I want to get high so high, Hits from the Bong!"

*

Dawn looked at Cha with venom in her eyes, "what do you mean huckled?"

Cha gave a little chuckle and responded, "You know arrested".

"I know what it means, what I'm wondering is whether or not I'll see him again?"

Cha smiled and said, "Its only just over a year. He may get time knocked off for good behaviour."

Dawn began to sob, "I really wanted to spend just a day or two with him."

"I know I know darling," said Mary as she cuddled her lassie. "Dry your eyes, dry your eyes. You'll pull through."

Cha looked on in dismay. He was sure that there was light at the end of this tunnel and he knew one thing that Grandad was in a shit storm of trouble, but Grandad being Grandad would pull through. He had keen survival instincts. No iron and concrete could pull a broomie boy down. No they were bred hard and fast. Knowing only that what came round the corner, be it friend or enemy could finish you with a knife to the guts. That's why so many YBC were loyal to the foil, be prepared, like the scouts only these boys were the scouts from Hell.

Cha piped up. "I'll try and get word to him so you can at least say goodbye over the telephone."

She smiled and lit a fag, "how long until I go to California mum?"

She smiled sweetly and replied, "end of this week."

Cha looked at the dusky wee bit and said. "That'll gie us plenty time." He then went down stairs and used the house phone.

"Kingo, it's me Cha, give me the number to McCrann's office."

Kingo looked up the lawyers number in his little black book that he used for tick.

"Thank you Kingo."

Kingo smiled and replied, "nae worries Cha I aim to please."

Cha then dialled McCrann.

"Hello McCrann Solicitors?"

Cha smiled, 'awright Doll I need to talk to your boss, and it's kinda urgent?"

"Who may I say is calling?"

"It's Charles Dunlop," He replied.

The phone went silent for a minute or two. Then Cha was put through.

"Hello Charlie how can I help?"

"Well Sir I need you to arrange a phone contact, For Leon as his girl is in bits about what happened."

McCrann smiled, "I'll see what I can do."

Cha knew from the sound in his voice that he was eager help. "Phone me tomorrow at about Two thirty I'll arrange everything for then."

Cha smiled. "Thank you," he said and McCrann replied. "Nae bother at all Charlie," they then hung up and Cha had a smoke out front of the House.

*

Grandad was a day into his incarceration and he was finally at the thought that the rat was going to win if he wasn't uncovered soon. Grandad was running out of time until he could set a trap. He was smiling as a half-ounce of GV was giving to him by a YO called Jimmy, Jimmy Gandhi. He spoke with the young lad who told him that he was down for a malicious wounding and subsequent death of friend of his over a shot of the puggy. In which he had seen red then took his pint of Guinness and thrust the fucking thing into the guys throat and face.

"So I needed To cool down, I never seen so much blood in my puff. You need dope or anything I'm your boy?"

Grandad smiled and said, "What about a CD player?"

Jimmy smiled and replied, "that sort of thing is considered governors discretion only at his say so. But I can put in a word for you."

Grandad smiled, "Any word about the war?"

Jimmy laughed, "I'll keep my heed down to hear every whisper and I'll keep you informed."

Grandad smiled and Jimmy giggled. "Grandad ae the YBC in here wae me." Shimmey smiled at Grandad who rolled a rollie and gave it tae Shimmey.

Giz showed face a couple of seconds later, "Oh I see you met Jimmy" said Gizmo who lit one as the other two did the same. "A bit of a pricey guy but he delivers, so they say."

Grandad looked on into the distance. When one of the screws came up to him, "Leon" he said as he drew nearer.

"Yes Boss," was the curt reply from Grandad.

"You've got a call coming in, some lassie, ring a bell?"

Grandad smiled and replied, "When?"

The screw looked the young casual up and down then spoke, "tonight after dinner." Grandad's face broke into a grin. He knew that Cha must have set it up.

"Thanks boss," said Grandad. The screw headed away and Grandad carried on with his smoke.

*

Cha and Raymie were just about through watching after Dawn, They would have to stick around until Dawn got on that plane to California. Then they could go back to Broomie. This would allow them to evaluate what damage had been done and how much recovery they would need. How much damage the polis had done. Dawn and Grandad had a good ten minutes on the phone, where they said their goodbyes and made promises to stay in touch via mail. Grandad's heart broke about a day or so later. Dawn's heart broke too. Cha and Raymie saw her off to America. Then headed away back through to Broomie. Straight up to Bats's house and straight into the stash. Bats smiled at the enthusiasm of the pair.

"I take it you'll be wanting a couple of bags of kit?" asked Bats as the two of them rolled a spliff each. Bats handed Cha a bag of smack and Raymie a bag as-well. They got nice and mellow. The police were still hunting the men that had done the damage on the four Leed's boys. Biscuit was recovering and Grandad, Shimmey and Gizmo got their heads down and did their time. They never did find the rat as they were too busy keeping things in perspective and knowing that more than a piece of cheese was needed to catch said rat they were just going to suffer as they knew that one day he would come to light.

The End